Microsoft®
PowerPoint® 2013

ILLUSTRATED

Brief | Introductory

David W. Beskeen

COURSE TECHNOLOGY
CENGAGE Learning·

Australia · Brazil · Japan · Korea · Mexico · Singapore · Spain · United Kingdom · United States

COURSE TECHNOLOGY
CENGAGE Learning

Microsoft® PowerPoint® 2013—Illustrated Brief
David W. Beskeen

Executive Editor: Marjorie Hunt

Associate Acquisitions Editor: Amanda Lyons

Senior Product Manager: Christina Kling-Garrett

Product Manager: Kim Klasner

Editorial Assistant: Brandelynn Perry

Brand Manager: Elinor Gregory

Developmental Editor: Rachel Biheller Bunin

Full-Service Project Management: GEX Publishing
Services

Copyeditor: Mark Goodin

Proofreader: Brandy Lilly

Indexer: Alexandra Nickerson

QA Manuscript Reviewers: John Freitas, Danielle
Shaw, Susan Whalen, Jeff Schwartz

Cover Designer: GEX Publishing Services

Cover Artist: GEX Publishing Services

Composition: GEX Publishing Services

For product information and technology assistance, contact us at
Cengage Learning Customer & Sales Support, 1-800-354-9706
For permission to use material from this text or product, submit all
requests online at **www.cengage.com/permissions**
Further permissions questions can be emailed to
permissionrequest@cengage.com

Library of Congress Control Number: 2013934312

ISBN-13: 978-1-285-08261-5
ISBN-10: 1-285-08261-3

Course Technology
20 Channel Center Street
Boston, MA 02210
USA

Cengage Learning is a leading provider of customized learning solutions with office locations around the globe, including Singapore, the United Kingdom, Australia, Mexico, Brazil, and Japan. Locate your local office at:
international.cengage.com/region

Cengage Learning products are represented in Canada by Nelson Education, Ltd.

To learn more about Course Technology, visit **www.cengage.com/coursetechnology**

To learn more about Cengage Learning, visit **www.cengage.com**

Purchase any of our products at your local college store or at our preferred online store
www.cengagebrain.com

Printed in the United States of America
1 2 3 4 5 6 7 19 18 17 16 15 14 13

Brief Contents

Contents

Preface

Welcome to Microsoft PowerPoint 2013—Illustrated Brief. This book has a unique design: each skill is presented on two facing pages, with steps on the left and screens on the right. The layout makes it easy to learn a skill without having to read a lot of text and flip pages to see an illustration.

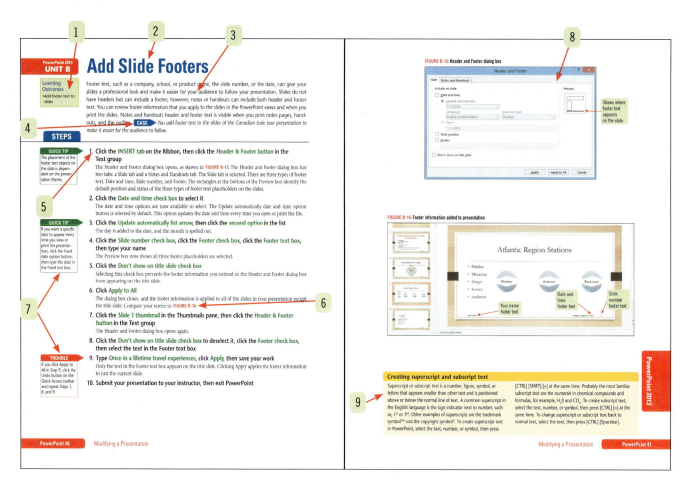

1 New! Learning Outcomes box lists measurable learning goals for which a student is accountable in that lesson.

2 Each two-page lesson focuses on a single skill.

3 Introduction briefly explains why the lesson skill is important.

4 A case scenario motivates the steps and puts learning in context.

5 Step-by-step instructions and brief explanations guide students through each hands-on lesson activity.

6 New! Figure references are now in red bold to help students refer back and forth between the steps and screenshots.

7 Tips and troubleshooting advice, right where you need it—next to the step itself.

8 New! Larger screen shots with green callouts keep students on track as they complete steps.

9 Clues to Use yellow boxes provide useful information related to the lesson skill.

This book is an ideal learning tool for a wide range of learners—the "rookies" will find the clean design easy to follow and focused with only essential information presented, and the "hotshots" will appreciate being able to move quickly through the lessons to find the information they need without reading a lot of text. The design also makes this a great reference after the course is over! See the illustration on the left to learn more about the pedagogical and design elements of a typical lesson.

What's New in this Edition

- **Coverage** — This book helps students learn essential skills using Microsoft PowerPoint 2013, including creating and modifying a presentation, inserting objects, and finalizing a presentation. The Working in the Cloud appendix helps students learn to use SkyDrive to save, share and manage files in the cloud and to use Office Web Apps.

- **New! Learning Outcomes** — Each lesson displays a green Learning Outcomes box that lists skills-based or knowledge-based learning goals for which students are accountable. Each Learning Outcome maps to a variety of learning activities and assessments. (See the *New! Learning Outcomes* section on page xii for more information.)

- **New! Updated Design** — This edition features many new design improvements to engage students — including larger lesson screenshots with green callouts and a refreshed Unit Opener page.

- **New! Independent Challenge 4: Explore** — This new case-based assessment activity allows students to explore new skills and use creativity to solve a problem or create a project.

Assignments

This book includes a wide variety of high quality assignments you can use for practice and assessment. Assignments include:

- **Concepts Review** — Multiple choice, matching, and screen identification questions.

- **Skills Review** — Step-by-step, hands-on review of every skill covered in the unit.

- **Independent Challenges 1-3** — Case projects requiring critical thinking and application of the unit skills. The Independent Challenges increase in difficulty. The first one in each unit provides the most hand-holding; the subsequent ones provide less guidance and require more critical thinking and independent problem solving.

- **Independent Challenge 4: Explore** — Case projects that let students explore new skills that are related to the core skills covered in the unit and are often more open ended, allowing students to use creativity to complete the assignment.

- **Visual Workshop** — Critical thinking exercises that require students to create a project by loking at a completed solution; they must apply the skills they've learned in the unit and use critical thinking skills to create the project from scratch.

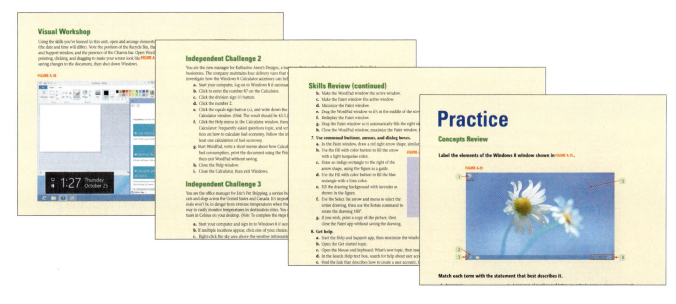

New! Learning Outcomes

Every 2-page lesson in this book now contains a green **Learning Outcomes box** that states the learning goals for that lesson.

- **What is a learning outcome?** A learning outcome states what a student is expected to know or be able to do after completing a lesson. Each learning outcome is skills-based or knowledge-based and is *measurable*. Learning outcomes map to learning activities and assessments.

- **How do students benefit from learning outcomes?** Learning outcomes tell students exactly what skills and knowledge they are *accountable* for learning in that lesson. This helps students study more efficiently and effectively and makes them more active learners.

- **How do instructors benefit from learning outcomes?** Learning outcomes provide clear, measurable, skills-based learning goals that map to various high-quality learning activities and assessments. A **Learning Outcomes Map**, available for each unit in this book, maps every learning outcome to the learning activities and assessments shown below.

Learning Outcomes Map to These Learning Activities:

1. **Book lessons:** Step-by-step tutorial on one skill presented in a two-page learning format
2. **Illustrated Videos:** Videos based on lessons in this book (sold separately on DVD, or in SAM)
3. **SAM Training:** Short animations and hands-on practice activities in simulated environment

Learning Outcomes Map to These Assessments:

1. **End-of-Unit Exercises: Concepts Review** (screen identification, matching, multiple choice); **Skills Review** (hands-on review of each lesson); **Independent Challenges** (hands-on, case-based review of specific skills); **Visual Workshop** (activity that requires student to build a project by looking at a picture of the final solution).
2. **Exam View Test Banks:** Objective-based questions you can use for online or paper testing.
3. **SAM Assessment:** Performance-based assessment in a simulated environment.
4. **SAM Projects:** Auto-graded projects for Word, Excel, Access, and PowerPoint that students create live in the application.
5. **Extra Independent Challenges:** Extra case-based exercises available in the Instructor Resources that cover various skills.

Learning Outcomes Map

A **Learning Outcomes Map**, contained in the Instructor Resources, provides a listing of learning activities and assessments for each learning outcome in the book.

Learning Outcomes Map
Microsoft Access 2013 Illustrated
Unit A--Getting Started with Microsoft Office 2013

KEY:
IC=Independent Challenge   EIC=Extra Independent Challenge
VW=Visual Workshop

	Concepts Review	Skills Review	IC1	IC2	IC3	IC4	VW	EIC 1	EIC 2	Test Bank	SAM Assessment	SAM Projects	SAM Training	Illustrated Video
Understand the Office 2013 Suite														
Identify Office suite components	✓		✓							✓				✓
Describe the features of each program			✓							✓				✓
Start an Office App														
Start an Office App			✓							✓	✓	✓	✓	✓
Explain the purpose of a template										✓				✓
Start a new blank document			✓							✓				✓
Identify Office 2013 Screen Elements														
Identify basic components of the user interface	✓									✓				✓
Display and use Backstage view			✓							✓				✓
Adjust the Zoom level	✓		✓							✓	✓	✓	✓	✓
Create and Save a File														
Create a file			✓							✓	✓	✓	✓	✓
Save a file	✓		✓							✓	✓	✓	✓	✓
Explain SkyDrive			✓							✓	✓	✓	✓	✓
Open a File and Save It with a New Name														
Open an existing file														✓

Online Learning and Assessment Tools

SAM

Get your students workplace-ready with SAM, the market-leading proficiency-based assessment and training solution for Microsoft Office! SAM's active, hands-on environment helps students master Microsoft Office skills and computer concepts that are essential to academic and career success, delivering the most comprehensive online learning solution for your course! Through skill-based assessments, interactive trainings, business-centric projects, and comprehensive remediation, SAM engages students in mastering the latest Microsoft Office programs on their own, giving instructors more time to focus on teaching. Computer concepts labs supplement instruction of important technology-related topics and issues through engaging simulations and interactive, auto-graded assessments. With enhancements including streamlined course setup, more robust grading and reporting features, and the integration of fully interactive MindTap Readers containing Cengage Learning's premier textbook and video content, SAM provides the best teaching and learning solution for your course. (SAM sold separately.)

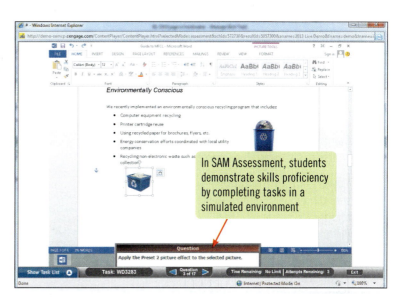

In SAM Assessment, students demonstrate skills proficiency by completing tasks in a simulated environment

Video Companion

Engage your students with videos! The *Video Companion for Microsoft Office 2013 Illustrated First Course* contains more than 150 videos based on the step-by-step lessons in our book *Microsoft Office 2013 Illustrated Introductory First Course*. Each video provides a multimedia version of a single two-page lesson in this text and includes a lesson overview along with a demonstration of the steps. Nearly 12 hours of videos provide instructional support. The Video Companion is a great learning tool for all students, and especially distance learning students or students who need help or reinforcement outside of the classroom. (Sold separately on DVD or in SAM MindTap Reader.)

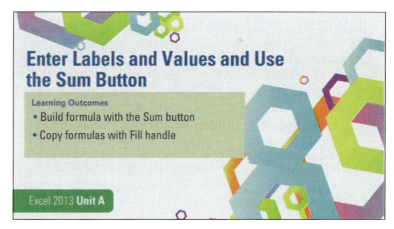

MindTap

MindTap is a fully online, highly personalized learning experience built upon Cengage Learning content. MindTap combines student learning tools—readings, multimedia, activities and assessments—into a singular Learning Path that guides students through their course. Instructors personalize the experience by customizing authoritative Cengage Learning content and learning tools, including the ability to add SAM trainings, assessments, and projects into the Learning Path via a SAM app that integrates into the MindTap framework seamlessly with Learning Management Systems. Available in 2014.

Instructor Resources

This book comes with a wide array of high-quality technology-based, teaching tools to help you teach and to help students learn. The following teaching tools are available for download at our Instructor Companion Site. Simply search for this text at *login.cengage.com*. An instructor login is required.

- **New! Learning Outcomes Map** — A detailed grid for each unit (in Excel format) shows the learning activities and assessments that map to each learning outcome in that unit.

- **Instructor's Manual** — Available as an electronic file, the Instructor's Manual includes lecture notes with teaching tips for each unit.

- **Sample Syllabus** — Prepare and customize your course easily using this sample course outline.

- **PowerPoint Presentations** — Each unit has a corresponding PowerPoint presentation covering the skills and topics in that unit that you can use in lectures, distribute to your students, or customize to suit your course.

- **Figure Files** — The figures in the text are provided on the Instructor Resources site to help you illustrate key topics or concepts. You can use these to create your own slide shows or learning tools.

- **Solution Files** — Solution Files are files that contain the finished project that students create or modify in the lessons or end-of-unit material.

- **Solutions Document** — This document outlines the solutions for the end-of-unit Concepts Review, Skills Review, Independent Challenges and Visual Workshops. An Annotated Solution File and Grading Rubric accompany each file and can be used together for efficient grading.

- **ExamView Test Banks** — ExamView is a powerful testing software package that allows you to create and administer printed, computer (LAN-based), and Internet exams. Our ExamView test banks include questions that correspond to the skills and concepts covered in this text, enabling students to generate detailed study guides that include page references for further review. The computer-based and Internet testing components allow students to take exams at their computers, and also save you time by grading each exam automatically.

Key Facts About Using This Book

Data Files are needed: To complete many of the lessons and end-of-unit assignments, students need to start from partially completed Data Files, which help students learn more efficiently. By starting out with a Data File, students can focus on performing specific tasks without having to create a file from scratch. All Data Files are available as part of the Instructor Resources. Students can also download Data Files themselves for free at cengagebrain.com. (For detailed instructions, go to www.cengage.com/ct/studentdownload.)

System requirements: This book was developed using Microsoft Office 2013 Professional running on Windows 8. Note that Windows 8 is not a requirement for the units on Microsoft Office; Office 2013 runs virtually the same on Windows 7 and Windows 8. Please see Important Notes for Windows 7 Users on the next page for more information.

Screen resolution: This book was written and tested on computers with monitors set at a resolution of 1366 x 768. If your screen shows more or less information than the figures in this book, your monitor is probably set at a higher or lower resolution. If you don't see something on your screen, you might have to scroll down or up to see the object identified in the figure.

Tell Us What You Think!

We want to hear from you! Please email your questions, comments, and suggestions to the Illustrated Series team at: **illustratedseries@cengage.com**

Important Notes for Windows 7 Users

The screenshots in this book show Microsoft Office 2013 running on Windows 8. However, if you are using Microsoft Windows 7, you can still use this book because Office 2013 runs virtually the same on both platforms. There are only two differences that you will encounter if you are using Windows 7. Read this section to understand the differences.

Dialog boxes

If you are a Windows 7 user, dialog boxes shown in this book will look slightly different than what you see on your screen. Dialog boxes for Windows 7 have a light blue title bar, instead of a medium blue title bar. However, beyond this superficial difference in appearance, the options in the dialog boxes across platforms are the same. For instance, the screen shots below in FIGURE 1 and FIGURE 2 show the Font dialog box running on Windows 7 and the Font dialog box running on Windows 8.

FIGURE 1: Font dialog box in Windows 7

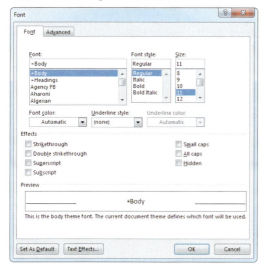

FIGURE 2: Font dialog box in Windows 8

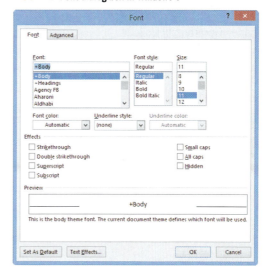

Alternate Steps for Starting an App in Windows 7

Nearly all of the steps in this book work exactly the same for Windows 7 users. However, starting an app (or program/application) requires different steps for Windows 7. The steps below show the Windows 7 steps for starting an app. (Note: Windows 7 alternate steps also appear in red Trouble boxes next to any step in the book that requires starting an app.)

Starting an app (or program/application) using Windows 7

1. Click the **Start button** on the taskbar to open the Start menu.
2. Click **All Programs**, then click the **Microsoft Office 2013 folder**. See Figure 3.
3. Click the app you want to use (such as **PowerPoint 2013**).

FIGURE 3: Starting an app using Windows 7

XV

Acknowledgements

Author Acknowledgements

Being a part of the extremely talented and experienced Office Illustrated team makes working on this book that much more enjoyable - many thanks to RBB, CKG, the production group, the testers, and the rest of the Cengage team!

–David W. Beskeen

Advisory Board Acknowledgements

We thank our Illustrated Advisory Board who gave us their opinions and guided our decisions as we developed this edition. They are as follows:

Merlin Amirtharaj, Stanly Community College

Londo Andrews, J. Sargeant Reynolds Community College

Rachelle Hall, Glendale Community College

Terri Helfand, Chaffey Community College

Sheryl Lenhart, Terra Community College

Dr. Jose Nieves, Lord Fairfax Community College

Getting Started with Microsoft Office 2013

CASE ▶ This unit introduces you to the most frequently used programs in Office, as well as common features they all share.

Unit Objectives

After completing this unit, you will be able to:

- Understand the Office 2013 suite
- Start an Office app
- Identify Office 2013 screen elements
- Create and save a file

- Open a file and save it with a new name
- View and print your work
- Get Help, close a file, and exit an app

File You Will Need

OFFICE A-1.xlsx

Understand the Office 2013 Suite

Learning Outcomes
- Identify Office suite components
- Describe the features of each program

Microsoft Office 2013 is a group of programs--which are also called applications or apps--designed to help you create documents, collaborate with coworkers, and track and analyze information. You use different Office programs to accomplish specific tasks, such as writing a letter or producing a presentation, yet all the programs have a similar look and feel. Microsoft Office 2013 apps feature a common, context-sensitive user interface, so you can get up to speed faster and use advanced features with greater ease. The Office apps are bundled together in a group called a **suite**. The Office suite is available in several configurations, but all include Word, Excel, and PowerPoint. Other configurations include Access, Outlook, Publisher, and other programs. **CASE** *As part of your job, you need to understand how each Office app is best used to complete specific tasks.*

DETAILS

The Office apps covered in this book include:

QUICK TIP

The terms "program" and "app" are used interchangeably.

- ### Microsoft Word 2013

  When you need to create any kind of text-based document, such as a memo, newsletter, or multipage report, Word is the program to use. You can easily make your documents look great by inserting eye-catching graphics and using formatting tools such as themes, which are available in most Office programs. **Themes** are predesigned combinations of color and formatting attributes you can apply to a document. The Word document shown in FIGURE A-1 was formatted with the Organic theme.

- ### Microsoft Excel 2013

  Excel is the perfect solution when you need to work with numeric values and make calculations. It puts the power of formulas, functions, charts, and other analytical tools into the hands of every user, so you can analyze sales projections, calculate loan payments, and present your findings in a professional manner. The Excel worksheet shown in FIGURE A-1 tracks personal expenses. Because Excel automatically recalculates results whenever a value changes, the information is always up to date. A chart illustrates how the monthly expenses are broken down.

- ### Microsoft PowerPoint 2013

  Using PowerPoint, it's easy to create powerful presentations complete with graphics, transitions, and even a soundtrack. Using professionally designed themes and clip art, you can quickly and easily create dynamic slide shows such as the one shown in FIGURE A-1.

- ### Microsoft Access 2013

  Access is a relational database program that helps you keep track of large amounts of quantitative data, such as product inventories or employee records. The form shown in FIGURE A-1 was created for a grocery store inventory database. Employees use the form to enter data about each item. Using Access enables employees to quickly find specific information such as price and quantity.

Microsoft Office has benefits beyond the power of each program, including:

QUICK TIP

In Word, Excel, and PowerPoint, the interface can be modified to automatically open a blank document, workbook, or presentation. To do this, click the FILE tab, click Options, click Show the Start screen when this application starts (to deselect it), then click OK. The next time the program opens, it will open a blank document.

- ### Common user interface: Improving business processes

  Because the Office suite programs have a similar **interface**, or look and feel, your experience using one program's tools makes it easy to learn those in the other programs. In addition, Office documents are **compatible** with one another, meaning that you can easily incorporate, or **integrate**, an Excel chart into a PowerPoint slide, or an Access table into a Word document.

- ### Collaboration: Simplifying how people work together

  Office recognizes the way people do business today, and supports the emphasis on communication and knowledge sharing within companies and across the globe. All Office programs include the capability to incorporate feedback—called **online collaboration**—across the Internet or a company network.

FIGURE A-1: Microsoft Office 2013 documents

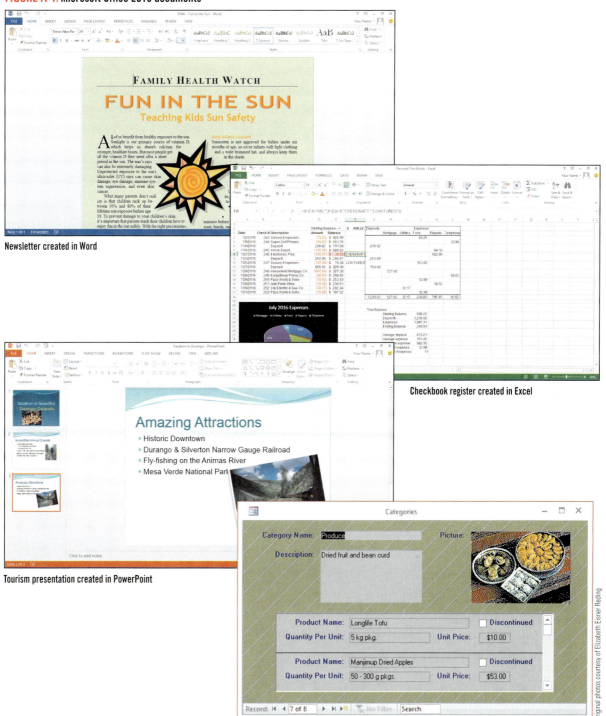

Newsletter created in Word

Checkbook register created in Excel

Tourism presentation created in PowerPoint

Store inventory form created in Access

What is Office 365?

Until the release of Microsoft Office 2013, most consumers purchased Microsoft Office in a traditional way: by buying a retail package from a store or downloading it from Microsoft. com. You can still purchase Microsoft Office 2013 in this traditional way--but you can also now purchase it as a subscription service called Microsoft Office 365 (for businesses) and Microsoft Office 365 Home Premium (for consumers). Office 365 requires businesses to pay a subscription fee for each user. Office 365 Home Premium Edition allows households to install Office on up to 5 devices. These subscription versions of Office provide extra services and are optimized for working in the cloud.

Start an Office App

Learning Outcomes
• Start an Office app
• Explain the purpose of a template
• Start a new blank document

To get started using Microsoft Office, you need to start, or **launch**, the Office app you want to use. If you are running Microsoft Office on Windows 8, an easy way to start the app you want is to go to the Start screen, type the app name you want to search for, then click the app name In the Results list. If you are running Windows 7, you start an app using the Start menu. (If you are running Windows 7, follow the Windows 7 steps at the bottom of this page.) **CASE** *You decide to familiarize yourself with Office by starting Microsoft Word.*

STEPS

1. **Go to the Windows 8 Start screen**

   Your screen displays a variety of colorful tiles for all the apps on your computer. You could locate the app you want to open by scrolling to the right until you see it, or you can type the app name to search for it.

2. **Type word**

   Your screen now displays "Word 2013" under "Results for 'word'", along with any other app that has "word" as part of its name (such as WordPad). See **FIGURE A-2**.

3. **Click Word 2013**

   Word 2013 launches, and the Word **start screen** appears, as shown in **FIGURE A-3**. The start screen is a landing page that appears when you first start an Office app. The left side of this screen displays recent files you have opened. (If you have never opened any files, then there will be no files listed under Recent.) The right side displays images depicting different templates you can use to create different types of documents. A **template** is a file containing professionally designed content that you can easily replace with your own. You can also start from scratch using the Blank Document option.

Starting an app using Windows 7

1. Click the Start button 🟦 on the taskbar
2. Click All Programs on the Start menu, click the Microsoft Office 2013 folder as shown in FIGURE A-4, then click Word 2013

Word 2013 launches, and the Word start screen appears, as shown previously in FIGURE A-3. The start screen is a landing page that appears when you first start an Office app. The left side of this screen displays recent files you have opened. (If you have never opened any files, then there will be no files listed under Recent.) The right side displays images depicting different templates you can use to create different types of documents. A **template** is a file containing professionally designed content that you can easily replace with your own. Using a template to create a document can save time and ensure that your document looks great. You can also start from scratch using the Blank Document option.

Using shortcut keys to move between Office programs

You can switch between open apps using a keyboard shortcut. The [Alt][Tab] keyboard combination lets you either switch quickly to the next open program or file or choose one from a gallery. To switch immediately to the next open program or file, press [Alt][Tab]. To choose from all open programs and files, press and hold [Alt], then press and release [Tab] without releasing [Alt]. A gallery opens on screen, displaying the filename and a thumbnail image of each open program and file, as well as of the desktop. Each time you press [Tab] while holding [Alt], the selection cycles to the next open file or location. Release [Alt] when the program, file, or location you want to activate is selected.

FIGURE A-2: Searching for Word app from the Start screen in Windows 8

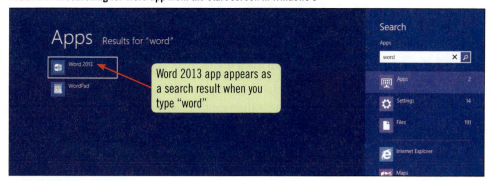

Word 2013 app appears as a search result when you type "word"

FIGURE A-3: Word start screen

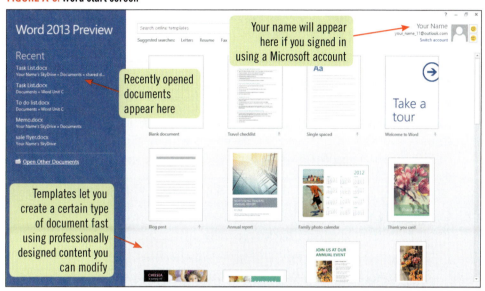

Your name will appear here if you signed in using a Microsoft account

Recently opened documents appear here

Templates let you create a certain type of document fast using professionally designed content you can modify

FIGURE A-4: Starting an app using Windows 7

Using the Office Clipboard

You can use the Office Clipboard to cut and copy items from one Office program and paste them into others. The Office Clipboard can store a maximum of 24 items. To access it, open the Office Clipboard task pane by clicking the dialog box launcher 🔲 in the Clipboard group on the HOME tab. Each time you copy a selection, it is saved in the Office Clipboard. Each entry in the Office Clipboard includes an icon that tells you the program it was created in. To paste an entry, click in the document where you want it to appear, then click the item in the Office Clipboard. To delete an item from the Office Clipboard, right-click the item, then click Delete.

Identify Office 2013 Screen Elements

One of the benefits of using Office is that the programs have much in common, making them easy to learn and making it simple to move from one to another. Individual Office programs have always shared many features, but the innovations in the Office 2013 user interface mean even greater similarity among them all. That means you can also use your knowledge of one program to get up to speed in another. A **user interface** is a collective term for all the ways you interact with a software program. The user interface in Office 2013 provides intuitive ways to choose commands, work with files, and navigate in the program window. **CASE** *Familiarize yourself with some of the common interface elements in Office by examining the PowerPoint program window.*

STEPS

1. **Go to the Windows 8 Start screen, type pow, click PowerPoint 2013, then click Blank Presentation**

   PowerPoint becomes the active program displaying a blank slide. Refer to **FIGURE A-5** to identify common elements of the Office user interface. The **document window** occupies most of the screen. At the top of every Office program window is a **title bar** that displays the document name and program name. Below the title bar is the **Ribbon**, which displays commands you're likely to need for the current task. Commands are organized onto **tabs**. The tab names appear at the top of the Ribbon, and the active tab appears in front.

2. **Click the FILE tab**

   The FILE tab opens, displaying **Backstage view**. It is called Backstage view becausee the commands available here are for working with the files "behind the scenes." The navigation bar on the left side of Backstage view contains commands to perform actions common to most Office programs.

3. **Click the Back button ⊙ to close Backstage view and return to the document window, then click the DESIGN tab on the Ribbon**

   To display a different tab, click its name. Each tab contains related commands arranged into **groups** to make features easy to find. On the DESIGN tab, the Themes group displays available design themes in a **gallery**, or visual collection of choices you can browse. Many groups contain a **dialog box launcher**, which you can click to open a dialog box or pane from which to choose related commands.

4. **Move the mouse pointer ▷ over the Ion theme in the Themes group as shown in FIGURE A-6, but *do not click* the mouse button**

   The Ion theme is temporarily applied to the slide in the document window. However, because you did not click the theme, you did not permanently change the slide. With the **Live Preview** feature, you can point to a choice, see the results, then decide if you want to make the change. Live Preview is available throughout Office.

5. **Move ▷ away from the Ribbon and towards the slide**

   If you had clicked the Ion theme, it would be applied to this slide. Instead, the slide remains unchanged.

6. **Point to the Zoom slider ⊟————│———⊞ 100% on the status bar, then drag to the right until the Zoom level reads 166%**

   The slide display is enlarged. Zoom tools are located on the status bar. You can drag the slider or click the Zoom In or Zoom Out buttons to zoom in or out on an area of interest. **Zooming in** (a higher percentage), makes a document appear bigger on screen but less of it fits on the screen at once; **zooming out** (a lower percentage) lets you see more of the document at a reduced size.

7. **Click the Zoom Out button ⊟ on the status bar to the left of the Zoom slider until the Zoom level reads 120%**

FIGURE A-5: PowerPoint program window

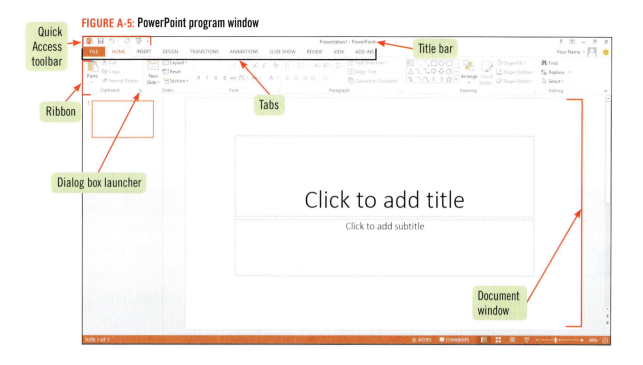

Quick Access toolbar

Ribbon

Dialog box launcher

Tabs

Title bar

Click to add title

Click to add subtitle

Document window

FIGURE A-6: Viewing a theme with Live Preview

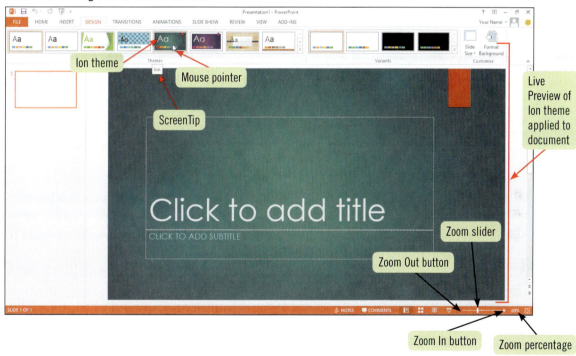

Ion theme

Mouse pointer

ScreenTip

Live Preview of Ion theme applied to document

Click to add title

CLICK TO ADD SUBTITLE

Zoom slider

Zoom Out button

Zoom In button

Zoom percentage

Using Backstage view

Backstage view in each Microsoft Office program offers "one stop shopping" for many commonly performed tasks, such as opening and saving a file, printing and previewing a document, defining document properties, sharing information, and exiting a program. Backstage view opens when you click the FILE tab in any Office program, and while features such as the Ribbon, Mini toolbar, and Live Preview all help you work *in* your documents, the FILE tab and Backstage view help you work *with* your documents. You can return to your active document by pressing the Back button.

Create and Save a File

Learning Outcomes
• Create a file
• Save a file
• Explain SkyDrive

When working in an Office program, one of the first things you need to do is to create and save a file. A **file** is a stored collection of data. Saving a file enables you to work on a project now, then put it away and work on it again later. In some Office programs, including Word, Excel, and PowerPoint, you can open a new file when you start the program, then all you have to do is enter some data and save it. In Access, you must create a file before you enter any data. You should give your files meaningful names and save them in an appropriate location, such as a folder on your hard drive or SkyDrive so they're easy to find. **SkyDrive** is the Microsoft cloud storage system that lets you easily save, share, and access your files from anywhere you have Internet access. See "Saving Files to SkyDrive" for more information on this topic. **CASE** ▶ *Use Word to familiarize yourself with creating and saving a document. First you'll type some notes about a possible location for a corporate meeting, then you'll save the information for later use.*

STEPS

1. Click the Word program button ⬛ on the taskbar, click Blank document, then click the Zoom In button ➕ until the level is 120%, if necessary

2. Type Locations for Corporate Meeting, then press [Enter] twice

   The text appears in the document window, and the **insertion point** blinks on a new blank line. The insertion point indicates where the next typed text will appear.

3. Type Las Vegas, NV, press [Enter], type San Diego, CA, press [Enter], type Seattle, WA, press [Enter] twice, then type your name

4. Click the Save button 🖫 on the Quick Access toolbar

   Backstage view opens showing various options for saving the file, as shown in **FIGURE A-7**.

5. Click Computer, then click Browse

   Because this is the first time you are saving this document, the Save As command is displayed. Once you choose a location where you will save the file, the Save As dialog box displays, as shown in **FIGURE A-8**. Once a file is saved, clicking 🖫 saves any changes to the file *without* opening the Save As dialog box. The Address bar in the Save As dialog box displays the default location for saving the file, but you can change it to any location. The File name field contains a suggested name for the document based on text in the file, but you can enter a different name.

6. Type OF A-Potential Corporate Meeting Locations

   The text you type replaces the highlighted text. (The "OF A-" in the filename indicates that the file is created in Office Unit A. You will see similar designations throughout this book when files are named.)

7. In the Save As dialog box, use the Address bar or Navigation Pane to navigate to the location where you store your Data Files

   You can store files on your computer, a network drive, your SkyDrive, or any acceptable storage device.

8. Click Save

   The Save As dialog box closes, the new file is saved to the location you specified, and the name of the document appears in the title bar, as shown in **FIGURE A-9**. (You may or may not see the file extension ".docx" after the filename.) See **TABLE A-1** for a description of the different types of files you create in Office, and the file extensions associated with each.

TABLE A-1: Common filenames and default file extensions

file created in	is called a	and has the default extension
Word	document	.docx
Excel	workbook	.xlsx
PowerPoint	presentation	.pptx
Access	database	.accdb

FIGURE A-7: Save As screen in Backstage view

Saves to your SkyDrive account

Click to save to your computer or alternate storage device

Click to change location for file

FIGURE A-8: Save As dialog box

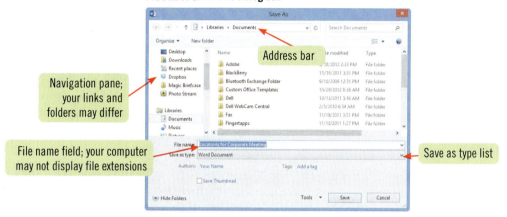

Address bar

Navigation pane; your links and folders may differ

File name field; your computer may not display file extensions

Save as type list

FIGURE A-9: Saved and named Word document

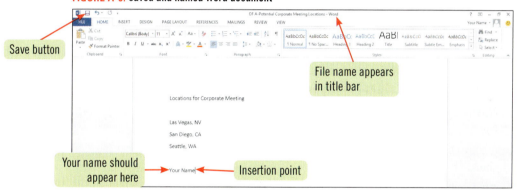

Save button

File name appears in title bar

Your name should appear here

Insertion point

Saving files to SkyDrive

All Office programs include the capability to incorporate feedback—called **online collaboration**—across the Internet or a company network. Using **cloud computing** (work done in a virtual environment), you can take advantage of commonly shared features such as a consistent interface. Using SkyDrive, a free file storage service from Microsoft, you and your colleagues can create and store documents in the cloud and make the documents available anywhere there is Internet access to whomever you choose. To use SkyDrive, you need a free Microsoft Account, which you obtain at the signup.live.com website. You can find more information about SkyDrive in the "Working in the Cloud" appendix. When you are logged into your Microsoft account and you save a file in any of the Office apps, the first option in the Save As screen is your SkyDrive. Double-click your SkyDrive option and the Save As dialog box opens displaying a location in the address bar unique to your SkyDrive account. Type a name in the File name text box, then click Save and your file is saved to your SkyDrive. To sync your files with SkyDrive, you'll need to download and install the SkyDrive for Windows app. Then, when you open Explorer, you'll notice a new folder called SkyDrive has been added to the Users folder. In this folder is a sub-folder called Documents, in which an updated copy of your Office app files resides. This means if your Internet connection fails, you can work on your files offline. The SkyDrive folder also displays Explorer in the list of Favorites folders.

Office 2013

Open a File and Save It with a New Name

Learning
Outcomes
• Open an existing
file
• Save a file with a
new name

In many cases as you work in Office, you start with a blank document, but often you need to use an existing file. It might be a file you or a coworker created earlier as a work in progress, or it could be a complete document that you want to use as the basis for another. For example, you might want to create a budget for this year using the budget you created last year; instead of typing in all the categories and information from scratch, you could open last year's budget, save it with a new name, and just make changes to update it for the current year. By opening the existing file and saving it with the Save As command, you create a duplicate that you can modify to suit your needs, while the original file remains intact. **CASE** *Use Excel to open an existing workbook file, and save it with a new name so the original remains unchanged.*

STEPS

TROUBLE
If you are running
WIndows 7, click
the Start button on
the taskbar, type
excel, then click
Excel 2013.

1. **Go to the Windows 8 Start screen, type exc, click Excel 2013, click Open Other Workbooks, click Computer on the navigation bar, then click Browse**

   The Open dialog box opens, where you can navigate to any drive or folder accessible to your computer to locate a file. You can click Recent Workbooks on the navigation bar to display a list of recent workbooks; click a file in the list to open it.

2. **In the Open dialog box, navigate to the location where you store your Data Files**

   The files available in the current folder are listed, as shown in **FIGURE A-10**. This folder displays one file.

TROUBLE
Click Enable Editing
on the Protected
View bar near the
top of your docu-
ment window if
prompted.

3. **Click OFFICE A-1.xlsx, then click Open**

   The dialog box closes, and the file opens in Excel. An Excel file is an electronic spreadsheet, so the new file displays a grid of rows and columns you can use to enter and organize data.

4. **Click the FILE tab, click Save As on the navigation bar, then click Browse**

   The Save As dialog box opens, and the current filename is highlighted in the File name text box. Using the Save As command enables you to create a copy of the current, existing file with a new name. This action preserves the original file and creates a new file that you can modify.

5. **Navigate to the location where you store your Data Files if necessary, type OF A-Budget for Corporate Meeting in the File name text box, as shown in FIGURE A-11, then click Save**

   A copy of the existing workbook is created with the new name. The original file, Office A-1.xlsx, closes automatically.

6. **Click cell A19, type your name, then press [Enter], as shown in FIGURE A-12**

   In Excel, you enter data in cells, which are formed by the intersection of a row and a column. Cell A19 is at the intersection of column A and row 19. When you press [Enter], the cell pointer moves to cell A20.

7. **Click the Save button 🔲 on the Quick Access toolbar**

   Your name appears in the workbook, and your changes to the file are saved.

Exploring File Open options

You might have noticed that the Open button in the Open dialog box includes a list arrow to the right of the button. In a dialog box, if a button includes a list arrow you can click the button to invoke the command, or you can click the list arrow to see a list of related commands that you can apply to a selected file in the file list. The Open list arrow includes several related commands, including Open Read-Only and Open as Copy.

Clicking Open Read-Only opens a file that you can only save with a new name; you cannot make changes to the original file. Clicking Open as Copy creates and opens a copy of the selected file and inserts the word "Copy" in the file's title. Like the Save As command, these commands provide additional ways to use copies of existing files while ensuring that original files do not get changed by mistake.

FIGURE A-10: Open dialog box

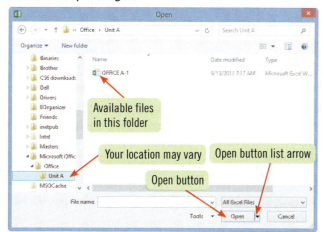

FIGURE A-11: Save As dialog box

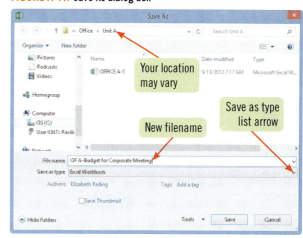

FIGURE A-12: Your name added to the workbook

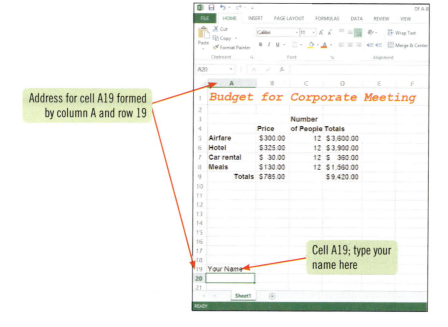

Working in Compatibility Mode

Not everyone upgrades to the newest version of Office. As a general rule, new software versions are **backward compatible**, meaning that documents saved by an older version can be read by newer software. To open documents created in older Office versions, Office 2013 includes a feature called Compatibility Mode. When you use Office 2013 to open a file created in an earlier version of Office, "Compatibility Mode" appears in the title bar, letting you know the file was created in an earlier but usable version of the program. If you are working with someone who may

not be using the newest version of the software, you can avoid possible incompatibility problems by saving your file in another, earlier format. To do this in an Office program, click the FILE tab, click Save As on the navigation bar, click the location where you want to save the file, then click Browse. In the Save As dialog box, click the Save as type list arrow in the Save As dialog box, then click an option on the list. For example, if you're working in Excel, click Excel 97-2003 Workbook format in the Save as type list to save an Excel file so it can be opened in Excel 97 or Excel 2003.

View and Print Your Work

Each Microsoft Office program lets you switch among various **views** of the document window to show more or fewer details or a different combination of elements that make it easier to complete certain tasks, such as formatting or reading text. Changing your view of a document does not affect the file in any way, it affects only the way it looks on screen. If your computer is connected to a printer or a print server, you can easily print any Office document using the Print button on the Print tab in Backstage view. Printing can be as simple as **previewing** the document to see exactly what a document will look like when it is printed and then clicking the Print button. Or, you can customize the print job by printing only selected pages. The Backstage view can also be used to share your document with others, or to export it in a different format. **CASE** *Experiment with changing your view of a Word document, and then preview and print your work.*

STEPS

1. **Click the Word program button on the taskbar**

   Word becomes the active program, and the document fills the screen.

2. **Click the VIEW tab on the Ribbon**

   In most Office programs, the VIEW tab on the Ribbon includes groups and commands for changing your view of the current document. You can also change views using the View buttons on the status bar.

3. **Click the Read Mode button in the Views group on the VIEW tab**

   The view changes to Read Mode view, as shown in **FIGURE A-13**. This view shows the document in an easy-to-read, distraction-free reading mode. Notice that the Ribbon is no longer visible on screen.

4. **Click the Print Layout button on the Status bar**

   You return to Print Layout view, the default view in Word.

5. **Click the FILE tab, then click Print on the navigation bar**

   The Print tab opens in Backstage view. The preview pane on the right side of the window displays a preview of how your document will look when printed. Compare your screen to **FIGURE A-14**. Options in the Settings section enable you to change margins, orientation, and paper size before printing. To change a setting, click it, and then click a new setting. For instance, to change from Letter paper size to Legal, click Letter in the Settings section, then click Legal on the menu that opens. The document preview updates as you change the settings. You also can use the Settings section to change which pages to print. If your computer is connected to multiple printers, you can click the current printer in the Printer section, then click the one you want to use. The Print section contains the Print button and also enables you to select the number of copies of the document to print.

6. **If your school allows printing, click the Print button in the Print section (otherwise, click the Back button)**

   If you chose to print, a copy of the document prints, and Backstage view closes.

Customizing the Quick Access toolbar

You can customize the Quick Access toolbar to display your favorite commands. To do so, click the Customize Quick Access Toolbar button in the title bar, then click the command you want to add. If you don't see the command in the list, click More Commands to open the Quick Access Toolbar tab of the current program's Options dialog box. In the Options dialog box, use the Choose commands from list to choose a category, click the desired command in the list on the left, click Add to add it to the Quick Access toolbar, then click OK. To remove a button from the toolbar, click the name in the list on the right in the Options dialog box, then click Remove. To add a command to the Quick Access toolbar as you work, simply right-click the button on the Ribbon, then click Add to Quick Access Toolbar on the shortcut menu. To move the Quick Access toolbar below the Ribbon, click the Customize Quick Access Toolbar button, and then click Show Below the Ribbon.

FIGURE A-13: Web Layout view

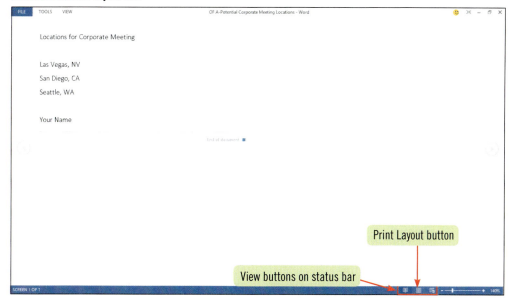

FIGURE A-14: Print settings on the FILE tab

Creating a screen capture

A **screen capture** is a digital image of your screen, as if you took a picture of it with a camera. For instance, you might want to take a screen capture if an error message occurs and you want a Technical Support person to see exactly what's on the screen. You can create a screen capture using features found in Windows 8 or Office 2013. Both Windows 7 and Windows 8 come with the Snipping Tool, a separate program designed to capture whole screens or portions of screens. To open the Snipping Tool, click the Start screen thumbnail, type "sni", then click the Snipping Tool when it appears in the left panel. After opening the Snipping Tool, click New, then drag the pointer on the screen to select the area of the screen you want to capture. When you release the mouse button, the screen capture opens in the Snipping Tool

window, and you can save, copy, or send it in an email. In Word, Excel, and PowerPoint 2013, you can capture screens or portions of screens and insert them in the current document using the Screenshot button in the Illustrations group on the INSERT tab. And finally, you can create a screen capture by pressing [PrtScn]. (Keyboards differ, but you may find the [PrtScn] button in or near your keyboard's function keys.) Pressing this key places a digital image of your screen in the Windows temporary storage area known as the **Clipboard**. Open the document where you want the screen capture to appear, click the HOME tab on the Ribbon (if necessary), then click the Paste button in the Clipboard group on the HOME tab. The screen capture is pasted into the document.

Get Help, Close a File, and Exit an App

You can get comprehensive help at any time by pressing [F1] in an Office app or clicking the Help button on the right end of the title bar. You can also get help in the form of a ScreenTip by pointing to almost any icon in the program window. When you're finished working in an Office document, you have a few choices regarding ending your work session. You close a file by clicking the FILE tab, then clicking Close; you exit a program by clicking the Close button on the title bar. Closing a file leaves a program running, while exiting a program closes all the open files in that program as well as the program itself. In all cases, Office reminds you if you try to close a file or exit a program and your document contains unsaved changes. **CASE** ▶ *Explore the Help system in Microsoft Office, and then close your documents and exit any open programs.*

STEPS

1. **Point to the Zoom button in the Zoom group on the VIEW tab of the Ribbon**

   A ScreenTip appears that describes how the Zoom button works and explains where to find other zoom controls.

2. **Click the Microsoft Word Help (F1) button ? in the upper-right corner of the title bar**

   The Word Help window opens, as shown in **FIGURE A-15**, displaying the home page for help in Word. Each entry is a hyperlink you can click to open a list of topics. The Help window also includes a toolbar of useful Help commands such as printing and increasing the font size for easier readability, and a Search field. If you are not connected to Office.com, a gold band is displayed telling you that you are not connected. Office.com supplements the help content available on your computer with a wide variety of up-to-date topics, templates, and training. If you are not connected to the Internet, the Help window displays only the help content available on your computer.

3. **Click the Learn Word basics link in the Getting started section of the Word Help window**

   The Word Help window changes, and a list of basic tasks appears below the topic.

4. **If necessary, scroll down until the Choose a template topic fills the Word Help window**

   The topic is displayed in the pane of the Help window, as shown in **FIGURE A-16**. The content in the window explains that you can create a document using a template (a pre-formatted document) or just create a blank document.

5. **Click in the Search online help text box, type Delete, then press [Enter]**

   The Word Help window now displays a list of links to topics about different types of deletions that are possible within Word.

6. **Click the Keep Help on Top button 📌 in the upper-right corner (below the Close button)**

   The Pin Help button rotates so the pin point is pointed towards the bottom of the screen: this allows you to read the Help window while you work on your document.

7. **Click the Word document window, then notice the Help window remains visible**

8. **Click a blank area of the Help window, click 📌 to Unpin Help, click the Close button ✕ in the Help window, then click the Close button ✕ in the upper-right corner of the screen**

   Word closes, and the Excel program window is active.

9. **Click the Close button ✕ to exit Excel, click the Close button ✕ to exit the remaining Excel workbook, click the PowerPoint program button 📊 on the taskbar if necessary, then click the Close button ✕ to exit PowerPoint**

   Excel and PowerPoint both close.

FIGURE A-15: Word Help window

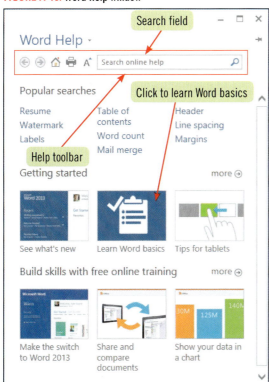

Search field

Click to learn Word basics

Help toolbar

FIGURE A-16: Create a document Help topic

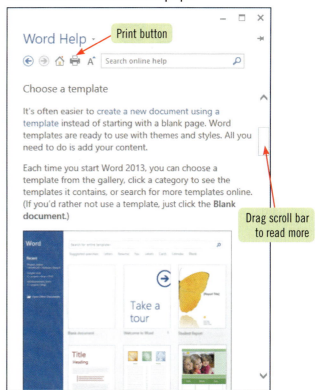

Print button

Drag scroll bar to read more

Enabling touch mode

If you are using a touch screen with any of the Office 2013 apps, you can enable the touch mode to give the user interface a more spacious look. Enable touch mode by clicking the Quick Access toolbar list arrow, then clicking Touch/Mouse Mode to select it. Then you'll see the Touch Mode button 🖐 in the Quick Access toolbar. Click 🖐, and you'll see the interface spread out.

Recovering a document

Each Office program has a built-in recovery feature that allows you to open and save files that were open at the time of an interruption such as a power failure. When you restart the program(s) after an interruption, the Document Recovery task pane opens on the left side of your screen displaying both original and recovered versions of the files that were open. If you're not sure which file to open (original or recovered), it's usually better to open the recovered file because it will contain the latest information. You can, however, open and review all versions of the file that were recovered and save the best one. Each file listed in the Document Recovery task pane displays a list arrow with options that allow you to open the file, save it as is, delete it, or show repairs made to it during recovery.

Office 2013

Practice

Concepts Review

Label the elements of the program window shown in FIGURE A-17.

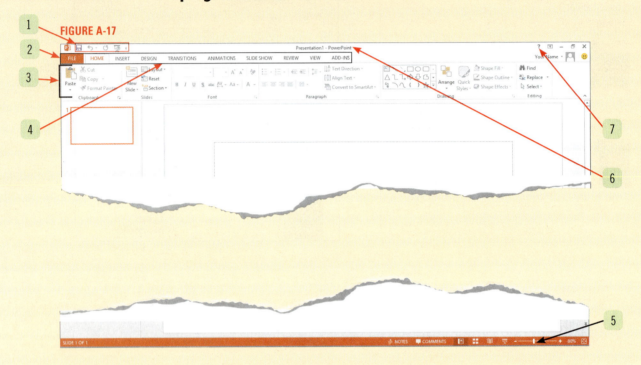

FIGURE A-17

Match each project with the program for which it is best suited.

8. Microsoft Access   a. Corporate convention budget with expense projections

9. Microsoft Excel   b. Presentation for city council meeting

10. Microsoft Word   c. Business cover letter for a job application

11. Microsoft PowerPoint   d. Department store inventory

Independent Challenge 1

You just accepted an administrative position with a local independently owned produce vendor that has recently invested in computers and is now considering purchasing Microsoft Office for the company. You are asked to propose ways Office might help the business. You produce your document in Word.

a. Start Word, create a new Blank document, then save the document as **OF A-Microsoft Office Document** in the location where you store your Data Files.

b. Change the zoom factor to 120%, type **Microsoft Word**, press [Enter] twice, type **Microsoft Excel**, press [Enter] twice, type **Microsoft PowerPoint**, press [Enter] twice, type **Microsoft Access**, press [Enter] twice, then type your name.

c. Click the line beneath each program name, type at least two tasks you can perform using that program (each separated by a comma), then press [Enter].

d. Save the document, then submit your work to your instructor as directed.

e. Exit Word.

Creating a Presentation in PowerPoint 2013

CASE Quest Specialty Travel (QST) is an adventure tour company that provides exclusive travel experiences for its clients. As a tour consultant for QST, one of your responsibilities is to research new vacation tours that QST can sell using the company Web site. You just finished investigating Canadian transcontinental train travel, and now you need to create a presentation using PowerPoint 2013 that describes the results of your research.

Unit Objectives

After completing this unit, you will be able to:

- Define presentation software
- Plan an effective presentation
- Examine the PowerPoint window
- Enter slide text

- Add a new slide
- Apply a design theme
- Compare presentation views
- Print a PowerPoint presentation

Files You Will Need

No files needed.

Define Presentation Software

Presentation software (also called presentation graphics software) is a computer program you use to organize and present information to others. Presentations are typically in the form of a slide show. Whether you are explaining a new product or moderating a meeting, presentation software can help you effectively communicate your ideas. You can use PowerPoint to create informational slides that you display, speaker notes for the presenter, and handouts for the audience. **CASE** *You need to start working on the Canadian train tours presentation. Because you are only somewhat familiar with PowerPoint, you get to work exploring its capabilities.* **FIGURE A-1** *shows how a presentation looks printed as handouts.* **FIGURE A-2** *shows how the same presentation might look printed as notes for a speaker.*

DETAILS

You can easily complete the following tasks using PowerPoint:

• **Enter and edit text easily**

Text editing and formatting commands in PowerPoint are organized by the task you are performing at the time, so you can enter, edit, and format text information simply and efficiently to produce the best results in the least amount of time.

• **Change the appearance of information**

PowerPoint has many effects that can transform the way text, graphics, and slides appear. By exploring some of these capabilities, you discover how easy it is to change the appearance of your presentation.

• **Organize and arrange information**

Once you start using PowerPoint, you won't have to spend much time making sure your information is correct and in the right order. With PowerPoint, you can quickly and easily rearrange and modify text, graphics, and slides in your presentation.

• **Include information from other sources**

Often, when you create presentations, you use information from a variety of sources. With PowerPoint, you can import text, photographs, numerical data, and facts from files created in programs such as Adobe Photoshop, Microsoft Word, Microsoft Excel, and Microsoft Access. You can also import information from other PowerPoint presentations as well as graphic images from a variety of sources such as the Internet, other computers, a digital camera, or other graphics programs. Always be sure you have permission to use any work that you did not create yourself.

• **Present information in a variety of ways**

With PowerPoint, you can present information using a variety of methods. For example, you can print handout pages or an outline of your presentation for audience members. You can display your presentation as an on-screen slide show using your computer, or if you are presenting to a large group, you can use a video projector and a large screen. If you want to reach an even wider audience, you can broadcast the presentation over the Internet so people anywhere in the world can use a Web browser to view your presentation.

• **Collaborate with others on a presentation**

PowerPoint makes it easy to collaborate or share a presentation with colleagues and coworkers using the Internet. You can use your email program to send a presentation as an attachment to a colleague for feedback. If you have a number of people that need to work together on a presentation, you can save the presentation to a shared workspace such as a network drive or SkyDrive so authorized users in your group with an Internet connection can access the presentation.

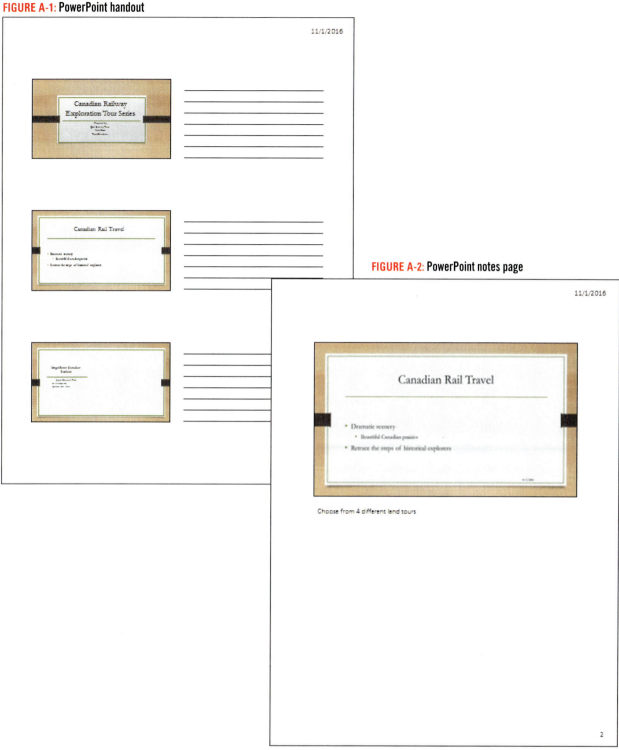

FIGURE A-1: PowerPoint handout

FIGURE A-2: PowerPoint notes page

Using PowerPoint on a touch screen

You can use PowerPoint 2013 on a Windows 8 computer with a touch-enabled monitor or any other compatible touch screen, such as a tablet computer. Using your fingers, you can use typical touch gestures to create, modify and navigate presentations. To enable touch mode capabilities in PowerPoint, you need to add the Touch Mode button to the Quick Access toolbar. Click the Customize Quick Access Toolbar button, click Touch/Mouse Mode, click the Touch/Mouse Mode button on the Quick Access toolbar then click Touch. In Touch mode, additional space is added around all of the buttons and icons in the Ribbon and the status bar to make them easier to touch. Common gestures that you can use in PowerPoint include double-tapping text to edit it and tapping a slide then dragging it to rearrange it in the presentation.

Plan an Effective Presentation

Before you create a presentation, you need to have a general idea of the information you want to communicate. PowerPoint is a powerful and flexible program that gives you the ability to start a presentation simply by entering the text of your message. If you have a specific design in mind that you want to use, you can start the presentation by working on the design. In most cases you'll probably enter the text of your presentation into PowerPoint first and then tailor the design to the message and audience. When preparing your presentation, you need to keep in mind not only who you are giving it to, but also how you are presenting it. For example, if you are giving a presentation using a projector, you need to know what other equipment you will need, such as a sound system and a projector. **CASE** ▶ *Use the planning guidelines below to help plan an effective presentation.* **FIGURE A-3** *illustrates a storyboard for a well-planned presentation.*

DETAILS

In planning a presentation, it is important to:

• **Determine and outline the message you want to communicate**

The more time you take developing the message and outline of your presentation, the better your presentation will be in the end. A presentation with a clear message that reads like a story and is illustrated with appropriate visual aids will have the greatest impact on your audience. Start the presentation by giving a general description of Canadian train travel and the types of tours offered by Quest Specialty Travel. See **FIGURE A-3**.

• **Identify your audience and where and how you are giving the presentation**

Audience and delivery location are major factors in the type of presentation you create. For example, a presentation you develop for a staff meeting that is held in a conference room would not necessarily need to be as sophisticated or detailed as a presentation that you develop for a large audience held in an auditorium. Room lighting, natural light, screen position, and room layout all affect how the audience responds to your presentation. You might also broadcast your presentation over the Internet to several people who view the presentation on their computers in real time. This presentation will be delivered in a small auditorium to QST's management and sales team.

• **Determine the type of output**

Output choices for a presentation include black-and-white or color handouts, on-screen slide show, or an online broadcast. Consider the time demands and computer equipment availability as you decide which output types to produce. Because you are speaking in a small auditorium to a large group and have access to a computer and projection equipment, you decide that an on-screen slide show is the best output choice for your presentation.

• **Determine the design**

Visual appeal, graphics, and presentation design work to communicate your message. You can choose one of the professionally designed themes that come with PowerPoint, modify one of these themes, or create one of your own. You decide to choose one of PowerPoint's design themes to convey the new tour information.

• **Decide what additional materials will be useful in the presentation**

You need to prepare not only the slides themselves but also supplementary materials, including speaker notes and handouts for the audience. You use speaker notes to help remember key details, and you pass out handouts for the audience to use as a reference during the presentation.

FIGURE A-3: Storyboard of the presentation

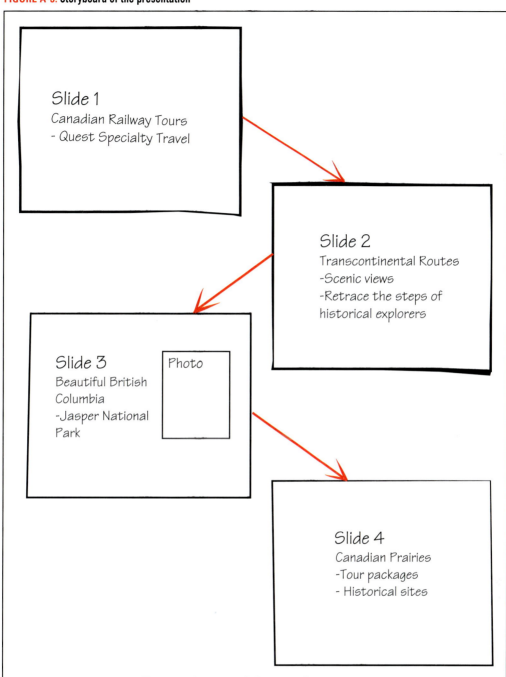

Slide 1
Canadian Railway Tours
- Quest Specialty Travel

Slide 2
Transcontinental Routes
-Scenic views
-Retrace the steps of
historical explorers

Slide 3
Beautiful British
Columbia
-Jasper National
Park

Photo

Slide 4
Canadian Prairies
-Tour packages
- Historical sites

Examine the PowerPoint Window

When you first start PowerPoint, you have the ability to choose what kind of presentation you want to use to start—a blank one, or one with a preformatted design. You can also open and work on an existing presentation. PowerPoint has different **views** that allow you to see your presentation in different forms. By default, the PowerPoint window opens in **Normal view**, which is the primary view that you use to write, edit, and design your presentation. Normal view is divided into two areas called **panes**: the pane on the left, called the Thumbnails pane, displays the slides of your presentation as small images, called **slide thumbnails**. The large pane is the Slide pane where you do most of your work on the slide. **CASE** *The PowerPoint window and the specific parts of Normal view are described below.*

STEPS

1. **Start PowerPoint 2013**

   PowerPoint starts and the PowerPoint start screen opens, as shown in **FIGURE A-4**.

2. **Click the Blank Presentation slide thumbnail**

   The PowerPoint window opens in Normal view as shown in **FIGURE A-5**.

DETAILS

Using Figure A-5 as a guide, examine the elements of the PowerPoint window, then find and compare the elements described below:

- The **Ribbon** is a wide band spanning the top of the PowerPoint window that organizes all of PowerPoint's primary commands. Each set of primary commands is identified by a **tab**; for example, the HOME tab is selected by default, as shown in **FIGURE A-5**. Commands are further arranged into **groups** on the Ribbon based on their function. So, for example, text formatting commands such as Bold, Underline, and Italic are located on the HOME tab, in the Font group.

- The **Thumbnails pane**. You can quickly navigate through the slides in your presentation by clicking the slide thumbnails on this pane. You can also add, delete, or rearrange slides using this pane.

- The **Slide pane** displays the current slide in your presentation.

- The **Quick Access toolbar** provides access to common commands such as Save, Undo, Redo, and Start From Beginning. The Quick Access toolbar is always visible no matter which Ribbon tab you select. This toolbar is fully customizable. Click the Customize Quick Access Toolbar button to add or remove buttons.

- The **View Shortcuts** buttons on the status bar allow you to switch quickly between PowerPoint views.

- The **Notes button** on the status bar allows you to open the Notes pane. The Notes pane is used to type text that references a slide's content. You can print these notes and refer to them when you make a presentation or print them as handouts and give them to your audience. The Notes pane is not visible to the audience when you show a slide presentation in Slide Show view.

- The **Comments button** on the status bar allows you to open the Comments pane. In the Comments pane you can create, edit, select, and delete comments.

- The **status bar**, located at the bottom of the PowerPoint window, shows messages about what you are doing and seeing in PowerPoint, including which slide you are viewing and the total number of slides. In addition, the status bar displays the Zoom slider controls, the Fit slide to current window button ⊞, and information on other functionality such as the presentation theme name, signatures and permissions.

- The **Zoom slider** is in the lower-right corner of the status bar and is used to zoom the slide in and out quickly.

FIGURE A-4: PowerPoint start screen

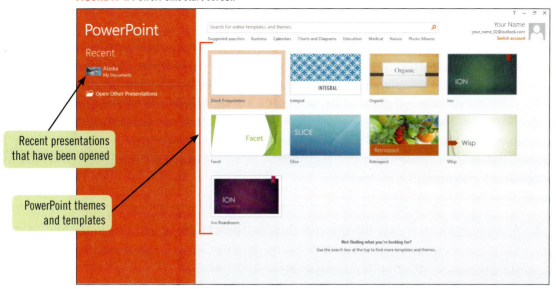

Recent presentations that have been opened

PowerPoint themes and templates

FIGURE A-5: PowerPoint window in Normal view

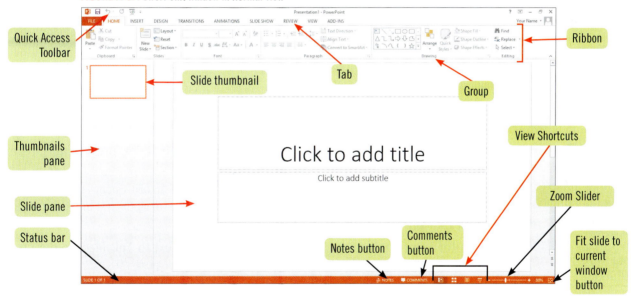

Quick Access Toolbar

Slide thumbnail

Tab

Ribbon

Group

Thumbnails pane

View Shortcuts

Slide pane

Zoom Slider

Status bar

Notes button

Comments button

Fit slide to current window button

Enter Slide Text

Learning Outcomes
• Enter slide text
• Change slide text

When you start a blank PowerPoint presentation, an empty title slide appears in Normal view. The title slide has two **text placeholders**—boxes with dotted borders—where you enter text. The top text placeholder on the title slide is the **title placeholder**, labeled "Click to add title". The bottom text placeholder on the title slide is the **subtitle text placeholder**, labeled "Click to add subtitle". To enter text in a placeholder, click the placeholder and then type your text. After you enter text in a placeholder, the placeholder becomes a text object. An **object** is any item on a slide that can be modified. Objects are the building blocks that make up a presentation slide. **CASE** ▶ *Begin working on your presentation by entering text on the title slide.*

STEPS

1. **Move the pointer** ⬚ **over the title placeholder labeled** Click to add title **in the Slide pane**

   The pointer changes to I when you move the pointer over the placeholder. In PowerPoint, the pointer often changes shape, depending on the task you are trying to accomplish.

2. **Click the** title placeholder **in the Slide pane**

   The **insertion point**, a blinking vertical line, indicates where your text appears when you type in the placeholder. A **selection box** with a dashed line border and **sizing handles** appears around the placeholder, indicating that it is selected and ready to accept text. When a placeholder or object is selected, you can change its shape or size by dragging one of the sizing handles. See **FIGURE A-6**.

TROUBLE
If you press a wrong key, press [Backspace] to erase the character.

3. **Type** Canadian Railway Exploration Tour Series

   PowerPoint wraps the text to a second line and then center-aligns the title text within the title placeholder, which is now a text object. Notice the text also appears on the slide thumbnail on the Thumbnails pane.

4. **Click the** subtitle text placeholder **in the Slide pane**

   The subtitle text placeholder is ready to accept text.

5. **Type** Presented by**, then press** [Enter]

   The insertion point moves to the next line in the text object.

QUICK TIP
To copy text, select the text, click the HOME tab, click the Copy button in the Clipboard group, place the insertion point, then click the Paste button in the Clipboard group.

6. **Type** Quest Specialty Tours**, press** [Enter]**, type** Adventure Tour Series**, press** [Enter]**, type your name, press** [Enter]**, then type** Tour Consultant

   Notice the AutoFit Options button ⬚ appears near the text object. The AutoFit Options button on your screen indicates that PowerPoint has automatically decreased the font size of all the text in the text object so it fits inside the text object.

7. **Click the** AutoFit Options button ⬚**, then click** Stop Fitting Text to This Placeholder **on the shortcut menu**

   The text in the text object changes back to its original size and no longer fits inside the text object.

8. **In the subtitle text object, position** I **to the right of** Series**, drag left to select the entire line of text, press** [Backspace]**, then click outside the text object in a blank area of the slide**

   The Adventure Tour Series line of text is deleted and the AutoFit Options button menu closes, as shown in **FIGURE A-7**. Clicking a blank area of the slide deselects all selected objects on the slide.

9. **Click the** Save button ⬚ **on the Quick Access toolbar to open Backstage view, then save the presentation as** PPT A-QST **in the location where you store your Data Files**

   In Backstage view, you have the option of saving your presentation to your computer or SkyDrive. Notice that PowerPoint automatically entered the title of the presentation as the filename in the Save As dialog box.

FIGURE A-6: Title text placeholder ready to accept text

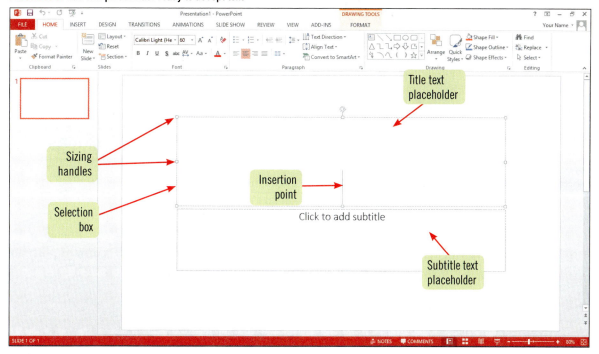

FIGURE A-7: Text on title slide

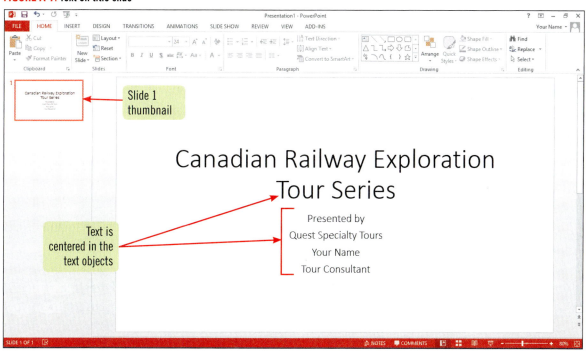

Saving fonts with your presentation

When you create a presentation, it uses the fonts that are installed on your computer. If you need to open the presentation on another computer, the fonts might look different if that computer has a different set of fonts. To preserve the look of your presentation on any computer, you can save, or embed, the fonts in your presentation. Click the FILE tab, then click Options. The PowerPoint Options dialog box opens. Click Save in the left pane, then click the Embed fonts in the file check box. Click the Embed all characters option button, then click OK to close the dialog box. Click Save on the Quick Access toolbar. Now the presentation looks the same on any computer that opens it. Using this option, however, significantly increases the size of your presentation, so only use it when necessary. You can freely embed any TrueType or OpenType font that comes with Windows. You can embed other TrueType fonts only if they have no license restrictions.

Add a New Slide

Learning Outcomes
• Add a new slide
• Indent text levels
• Modify slide layout

Usually when you add a new slide to a presentation, you have a pretty good idea of what you want the slide to look like. For example, you may want to add a slide that has a title over bulleted text and a picture. To help you add a slide like this quickly and easily, PowerPoint provides nine standard slide layouts. A **slide layout** contains text and object placeholders that are arranged in a specific way on the slide. You have already worked with the Title Slide layout in the previous lesson. In the event that a standard slide layout does not meet your needs, you can modify an existing slide layout or create a new, custom slide layout. **CASE** ▶ *To continue developing the presentation, you create a slide that defines the new tour series.*

STEPS

1. **Click the New Slide button in the Slides group on the HOME tab on the Ribbon**

   A new blank slide (now the current slide) appears as the second slide in your presentation, as shown in **FIGURE A-8**. The new slide contains a title placeholder and a content placeholder. A **content placeholder** can be used to insert text or objects such as tables, charts, or pictures. Notice the status bar indicates Slide 2 of 2 and the Thumbnails pane now contains two slide thumbnails.

2. **Type Canadian Rail Travel, then click the bottom content placeholder**

   The text you typed appears in the title placeholder, and the insertion point is now at the top of the bottom content placeholder.

3. **Type Dramatic scenery, then press [Enter]**

   The insertion point appears directly below the text when you press [Enter], and a new first-level bullet automatically appears.

4. **Press [Tab]**

   The new first-level bullet is indented and becomes a second-level bullet.

QUICK TIP
You can also press [Shift][Tab] to decrease the indent level.

5. **Type Beautiful Canadian prairies, press [Enter], then click the Decrease List Level button ⇤ in the Paragraph group**

   The Decrease List Level button changes the second-level bullet into a first-level bullet.

6. **Type Retrace the steps of historical explorers, then click the New Slide list arrow in the Slides group**

   The Office Theme layout gallery opens. Each slide layout is identified by a descriptive name.

7. **Click the Content with Caption slide layout, then type Magnificent Canadian Rockies**

   A new slide with three content placeholders appears as the third slide. The text you typed is the title text for the slide.

8. **Click the lower-left placeholder, type Jasper National Park, press [Enter], click the Increase List Level button ⇥, type Visit the Maligne Valley, press [Enter], then type Spectacular wildlife scenes**

   The Increase List Level button moves the insertion point one level to the right. Notice this text placeholder does not use text bullets to identify separate lines of text.

9. **Click a blank area of the slide, then click the Save button 🖫 on the Quick Access toolbar**

   The Save button saves all of the changes to the file. Compare your screen with **FIGURE A-9**.

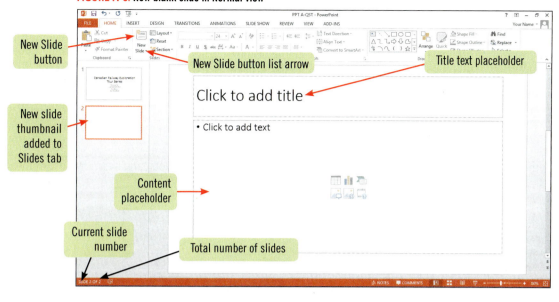

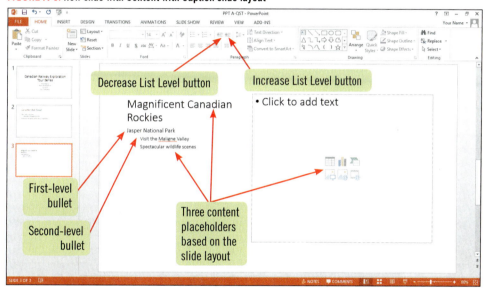

Entering and printing notes

You can add notes to your slides when there are certain facts you want to remember during a presentation or when there is additional information you want to hand out to your audience. Notes do not appear on the slides when you run a slide show. Use the Notes pane in Normal view or Notes Page view to enter notes for your slides. To open or close the Notes pane, click the Notes button on the status bar. To enter text notes on a slide, click in the Notes pane, then type. If you want to insert graphics as notes, you must use Notes Page view. To open Notes Page view, click the VIEW tab on the Ribbon, then click the Notes Page button in the Presentation Views group. You can print your notes by clicking the FILE tab on the Ribbon to open Backstage view, then clicking Print. Click the Full Page Slides list arrow in the Settings group (this button retains the last setting for what was printed previously so it might differ) to open the gallery, and then click Notes Pages. Once you verify your print settings, click the Print button. If you don't enter any notes in the Notes pane, and print the notes pages, the slides print as large thumbnails with blank space below the thumbnails to hand write notes.

PowerPoint 2013

Creating a Presentation in PowerPoint 2013

Apply a Design Theme

PowerPoint provides many design themes to help you quickly create a professional and contemporary looking presentation. A **theme** includes a set of 12 coordinated colors for text, fill, line, and shadow, called **theme colors**; a set of fonts for titles and other text, called **theme fonts**; and a set of effects for lines and fills, called **theme effects** to create a cohesive look. Each theme has at least four custom coordinated variants that provides you with additional color options. In most cases, you would apply one theme to an entire presentation; you can, however, apply multiple themes to the same presentation or even a different theme on each presentation slide. You can use a design theme as is, or you can alter individual elements of the theme as needed. Unless you need to use a specific design theme, such as a company theme or product design theme, it is faser and easier to use one of the themes supplied with PowerPoint. If you design a custom theme, you can save it to use in the future. **CASE** *You decide to change the default design theme in the presentation to a new one.*

STEPS

1. **Click the Slide 1 thumbnail on the Thumbnails pane**

   Slide 1, the title slide, appears in the Slide pane.

2. **Click the DESIGN tab on the Ribbon, then point to the Facet theme in the Themes group as shown in FIGURE A-10**

   The DESIGN tab appears, and a Live Preview of the Facet theme is displayed on the selected slide. A **Live Preview** allows you to see how your changes affect the slides before actually making the change. The Live Preview lasts about 1 minute, and then your slide reverts back to its original state. The first (far left) theme thumbnail identifies the current theme applied to the presentation, in this case, the default design theme called the Office Theme. Depending on your monitor resolution and screen size, you can see between four and 21 design themes in the Themes group.

3. **Slowly move your pointer ▷ over the other design themes, then click the Themes group down scroll arrow**

   A Live Preview of the theme appears on the slide each time you pass your pointer over the theme thumbnails, and a ScreenTip identifies the theme names.

4. **Move ▷ over the design themes, then click the Wisp theme**

   The Wisp design theme is applied to all the slides in the presentation. Notice the new slide background color, graphic elements, fonts, and text color. You decide this theme isn't right for this presentation.

5. **Click the More button ▾ in the Themes group**

   The Themes gallery window opens. At the top of the gallery window in the This Presentation section is the current theme applied to the presentation. Notice that just the Wisp theme is listed here because when you changed the theme in the last step, you replaced the default theme with the Wisp theme. The Office section identifies all 21 of the standard themes that come with PowerPoint.

6. **Right-click the Organic theme in the Office section, then click Apply to Selected Slides**

   The Organic theme is applied only to Slide 1. You like the Organic theme better, and decide to apply it to all slides.

7. **Right-click the Organic theme in the Themes group, then click Apply to All Slides**

   The Organic theme is applied to all three slides. Preview the next slides in the presentation to see how it looks.

8. **Click the Next Slide button ▼ at the bottom of the vertical scroll bar**

   Compare your screen to FIGURE A-11.

9. **Click the Previous Slide button ▲ at the bottom of the vertical scroll bar, then save your changes**

Creating a Presentation in PowerPoint 2013

FIGURE A-10: Slide showing a different design theme

Current theme applied
DESIGN tab
Office theme
Facet theme
Screentip
More button
Themes group down scroll arrow
Variants
New font type
New graphic elements

Canadian Railway Exploration Tour Series

Presented by
Quest Specialty Tours
Your Name
Tour Consultant

FIGURE A-11: Presentation with Organic theme applied

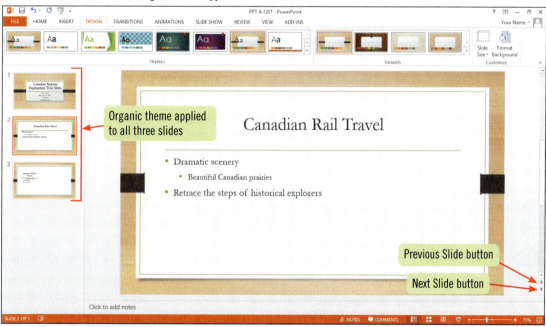

Organic theme applied to all three slides
Previous Slide button
Next Slide button

Canadian Rail Travel

• Dramatic scenery
  • Beautiful Canadian prairies
• Retrace the steps of historical explorers

Click to add notes

Customizing themes

You are not limited to using the standard themes PowerPoint provides; you can also modify a theme to create your own custom theme. For example, you might want to incorporate your school's or company's colors on the slide background of the presentation or be able to type using fonts your company uses for brand recognition. To change an existing theme, click the VIEW tab on the Ribbon, then click one of the Master buttons in the Master Views group. Click the Theme Colors button, the Theme Fonts button, or the Theme Effects button in the Background group to make changes to the theme, then save this new theme for future use by clicking the Themes button in the Edit Themes group, then click Save Current Theme. You also have the ability to create a new font theme or color theme from scratch by clicking the Theme Fonts button or the Theme Colors button and then clicking Customize Fonts or Customize Colors. You work in the Create New Theme Fonts or Create New Theme Colors dialog box to define the custom theme fonts or colors.

Compare Presentation Views

PowerPoint has six primary views: Normal view, Outline view, Slide Sorter view, Notes Page view, Slide Show view, and Reading view. Each PowerPoint view displays your presentation in a different way and is used for different purposes. Normal view is the primary editing view where you add text, graphics, and other elements to the slides. Outline view is the view you use to focus on the text of your presentation. Slide Sorter view is primarily used to rearrange slides; however, you can also add slide effects and design themes in this view. You use Notes Page view to type notes that are important for each slide. Slide Show view displays your presentation over the whole computer screen and is designed to show your presentation to an audience. Similar to Slide Show view, Reading view is designed to view your presentation on a computer screen. To move easily among the PowerPoint views, use the View Shortcuts buttons located on the status bar and the VIEW tab on the Ribbon. **TABLE A-1** provides a brief description of the PowerPoint views. **CASE** ▶ *Examine each of the PowerPoint views, starting with Normal view.*

STEPS

1. **Click the VIEW tab on the Ribbon, then click the Outline View button in the Presentation Views group**

   The presentation text is in the Outline pane on the left side of the window as shown in **FIGURE A-12**. Notice the status bar identifies the number of the slide you are viewing and the total number of slides in the presentation.

2. **Click the small slide icon ☐ next to Slide 2 in the Outline pane, then click the Slide Sorter button ⊞ on the status bar**

   Slide Sorter View opens to display a thumbnail of each slide in the presentation in the window. You can examine the flow of your slides and drag any slide or group of slides to rearrange the order of the slides in the presentation.

3. **Double-click the Slide 1 thumbnail, then click the Reading View button 📖 on the status bar**

   The first slide fills the screen as shown in **FIGURE A-13**. Use Reading view to review your presentation or to show your presentation to someone directly on your computer. The status bar controls at the bottom of the window make it easy to move between slides in this view.

4. **Click the Slide Show button 🖵 on the status bar**

   The first slide fills the entire screen now without the title bar and status bar. In this view, you can practice running through your slides as they would appear in a slide show.

5. **Click the left mouse button to advance through the slides one at a time until you see a black slide, then click once more to return to Outline view**

   The black slide at the end of the slide show indicates the slide show is finished. At the end of a slide show you automatically return to the slide and PowerPoint view you were in before you ran the slide show, in this case Slide 1 in Outline view.

6. **Click the Notes Page button in the Presentation Views group**

   Notes Page view appears, showing a reduced image of the current slide above a large text placeholder. You can enter text in this placeholder and then print the notes page for your own use.

7. **Click the Normal button in the Presentation Views group, then click the HOME tab on the Ribbon**

Creating a Presentation in PowerPoint 2013

FIGURE A-12: Outline view

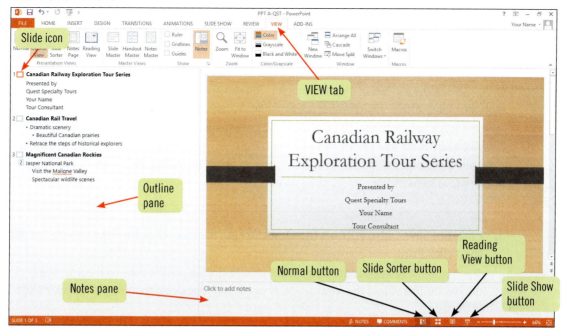

FIGURE A-13: Reading view

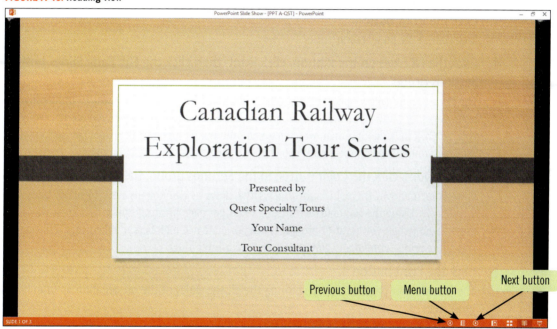

TABLE A-1: PowerPoint views

view name	button	button name	displays
Normal	▣	Normal	The Slide pane and the thumbnails pane at the same time
Outline View	(no View Shortcuts button)		An outline of the presentation and the Slide pane at the same time
Slide Sorter	▦	Slide Sorter	Thumbnails of all slides
Slide Show	▭	Slide Show	Your presentation on the whole computer screen
Reading View	▥	Reading View	Your presentation in a large window on your computer screen
Notes Page	(no View Shortcuts button)		A reduced image of the current slide above a large text box

PowerPoint 2013

Print a PowerPoint Presentation

Learning Outcomes
- Print a presentation
- Set print settings
- Modify color settings

You print your presentation when you want to review your work or when you have completed it and want a hard copy. Reviewing your presentation at different stages of development gives you a better perspective of the overall flow and feel of the presentation. You can also preview your presentation to see exactly how each slide looks before you print the presentation. When you are finished working on your presentation, even if it is not yet complete, you can close the presentation file and exit PowerPoint. **CASE** *You are done working on the tour presentation for now. You save and preview the presentation, then you print the slides and notes pages of the presentation so you can review them later. Before leaving for the day, you close the file and exit PowerPoint.*

STEPS

1. **Click the Save button** 🖫 **on the Quick Access toolbar, click the FILE tab on the Ribbon, then click Print**

   The Print window opens as shown in **FIGURE A-14**. Notice the preview pane on the right side of the window displays the first slide of the presentation. If you do not have a color printer, you will see a grayscale image of the slide.

   QUICK TIP
   To quickly print the presentation with the current Print options, add the Quick Print button to the Quick Access toolbar.

2. **Click the Next Page button** ▶ **at the bottom of the Preview pane, then click** ▶ **again**

   Each slide in the presentation appears in the preview pane.

3. **Click the Print button**

   Each slide in the presentation prints.

4. **Click the FILE tab on the Ribbon, click Print, then click the Full Page Slides button in the Settings group**

   The Print Layout gallery opens. In this gallery you can specify what you want to print (slides, handouts, notes pages, or outline), as well as other print options. To save paper when you are reviewing your slides, you can print in handout format, which lets you print up to nine slides per page. The options you choose in the Print window remain there until you change them or close the presentation.

   QUICK TIP
   To print slides appropriate in size for overhead transparencies, click the DESIGN tab, click the Slide Size button in the Customize group, click Customize Slide Size, click the Slides sized for list arrow, then click Overhead.

5. **Click 3 Slides, click the Color button in the Settings group, then click Pure Black and White**

   PowerPoint removes the color and displays the slides as thumbnails next to blank lines as shown in **FIGURE A-15**. Using the Handouts with three slides per page printing option is a great way to print your presentation when you want to provide a way for audience members to take notes. Printing pure black-and-white prints without any gray tones can save printer toner.

6. **Click the Print button**

   The presentation prints one page showing the all the slides of the presentation as thumbnails next to blank lines.

7. **Click the FILE tab on the Ribbon, then click Close**

   If you have made changes to your presentation, a Microsoft PowerPoint alert box opens asking you if you want to save changes you have made to your presentation file.

8. **Click Save, if necessary, to close the alert box**

   Your presentation closes.

9. **Click the Close button** ⊠ **in the Title bar**

   The PowerPoint program closes, and you return to the Windows desktop.

FIGURE A-14: Print window

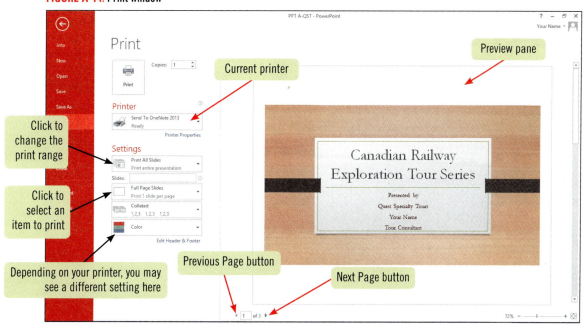

FIGURE A-15: Print window with changed settings

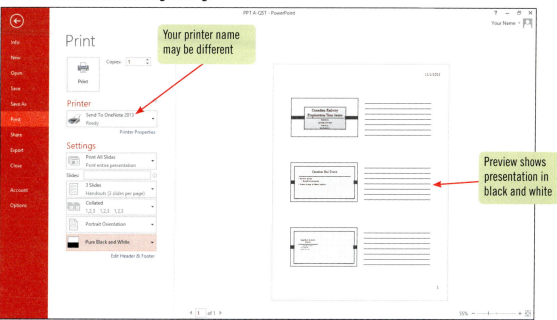

Microsoft Office Web Apps

All Office programs include the capability to incorporate feed-back—called online collaboration—across the Internet or a company network. Using **cloud computing** (work done in a virtual environment), you can take advantage of Web programs called Microsoft Office Web Apps, which are simplified versions of the programs found in the Microsoft Office 2013 suite. Because these programs are online, they take up no computer disk space and are accessed using Microsoft SkyDrive, a free service from Microsoft. Using Microsoft SkyDrive, you and your colleagues can create and store documents in the "cloud" and make the documents available to whomever you grant access. To use Microsoft SkyDrive, you need to create a free Microsoft account and establish a Windows Live ID, which you obtain at the Microsoft web site. You can find more information in the "Working in the Cloud" appendix.

Practice

Concepts Review

Label each element of the PowerPoint window shown in FIGURE A-16.

FIGURE A-16

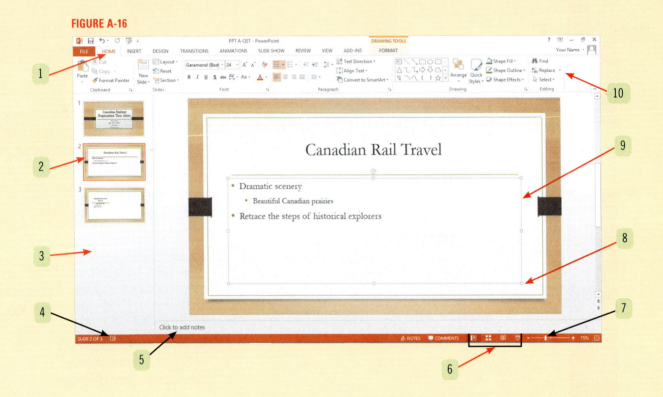

Match each term with the statement that best describes it.

11. Sizing handle
12. Slide Show view
13. Theme
14. Zoom slider
15. Reading view
16. Slide Layout

a. Placeholders arranged in a specific way on the slide
b. Used to change the size of an object
c. A view that is used to review a presentation or to show someone a presentation directly on a computer screen
d. A view that displays a presentation to show to an audience
e. Set of coordinated colors, fonts, and effects
f. Allows you to change the size of the slide in the window

Select the best answer from the list of choices.

17. **Which statement about PowerPoint is *not* correct?**
    a. Graphic images from a digital camera can be inserted into PowerPoint.
    b. A presentation can be broadcast over the Internet.
    c. You can use PowerPoint to create a database of information.
    d. You can import text and numerical data into PowerPoint.

18. **Which feature on the status bar allows you to quickly switch between views?**
    a. Fit slide to current window button
    b. Switch view button
    c. Zoom Slider
    d. View Shortcuts

19. **Finish the following sentence: "Copyright attaches to any original work of authorship,...":**
    a. After you register it with the Copyright Office.
    b. As soon as it is created.
    c. Under the Fair Use policy.
    d. Only when it displays the copyright symbol ©.

20. **Other than the Slide pane, where else can you enter slide text?**
    a. Outline view
    b. Slides tab
    c. Reading pane
    d. Notes Page view

21. **According to this unit, what are the building blocks of a presentation?**
    a. Slides
    b. Graphics
    c. Placeholders
    d. Objects

22. **The view that fills the entire screen with each slide in the presentation including the title bar is called:**
    a. Slide Show view.
    b. Fit to window view.
    c. Reading view.
    d. Normal view.

23. **Which of the following is not included in a design theme?**
    a. Fonts
    b. Colors
    c. Pictures
    d. Normal view

24. **What is the function of the slide layout?**
    a. Puts all your slides in order.
    b. Shows you which themes you can apply.
    c. Defines how all the elements on a slide are arranged.
    d. Enables you to apply a template to the presentation.

Skills Review

1. **Examine the PowerPoint window.**
    a. Start PowerPoint, if necessary then open a new blank presentation.
    b. Identify as many elements of the PowerPoint window as you can without referring to the unit material.
    c. Be able to describe the purpose or function of each element.
    d. For any elements you cannot identify, refer to the unit.

2. **Enter slide text.**
    a. In the Slide pane in Normal view, enter the text **Historic Hendra Stamp Mill & Hotel** in the title placeholder.
    b. In the subtitle text placeholder, enter **Nevada Ghost Town Preservation Society**.
    c. On the next line of the placeholder, enter your name.
    d. Deselect the text object.
    e. Save the presentation using the filename **PPT A-Dun Glen** to location where you store your Data Files.

Skills Review (continued)

3. Add a new slide.

  a. Create a new slide.

  b. Using FIGURE A-17, enter text on the slide.

  c. Create another new slide.

  d. Using FIGURE A-18, enter text on the slide.

  e. Save your changes.

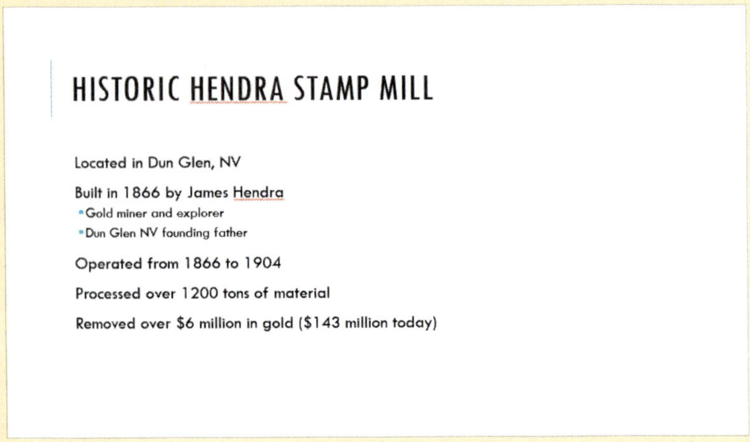

4. Apply a design theme.

  a. Click the DESIGN tab.

  b. Click the Themes group More button, then point to all of the themes.

  c. Locate the Slice theme, then apply it to the selected slide.

  d. Select Slide 1.

  e. Locate the Integral theme, then apply it to Slide 1.

  f. Apply the Integral theme to all of the slides in the presentation.

  g. Use the Next Slide button to move to Slide 3, then save your changes.

5. Compare presentation views.

  a. Click the VIEW tab, then click the Outline View button in the Presentation Views group.

  b. Click the Slide Sorter button in the Presentation Views group.

  c. Click the Notes Page button in the Presentation Views group, then click the Previous Slide button twice.

  d. Click the Reading View button in the Presentation Views group, then click the Next button on the status bar.

  e. Click the Normal button on the status bar, then click the Slide Show button.

  f. Advance the slides until a black screen appears, then click to end the presentation.

  g. Save your changes.

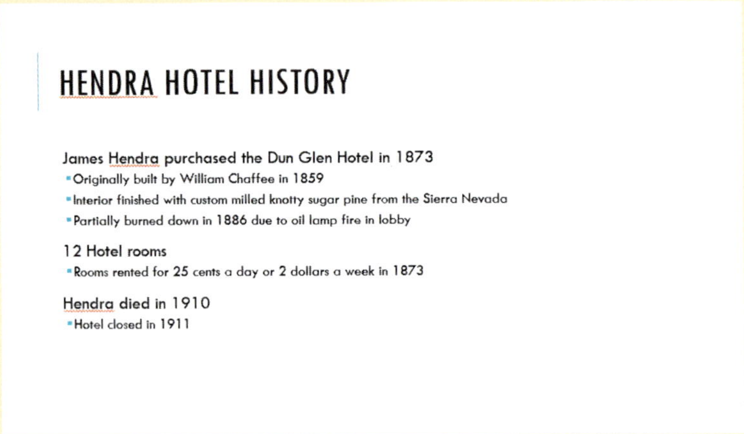

6. Print a PowerPoint presentation.

  a. Print all the slides as handouts, 4 Slides Horizontal, in color.

  b. Print the presentation outline.

  c. Close the file, saving your changes.

  d. Exit PowerPoint.

FIGURE A-17

HISTORIC HENDRA STAMP MILL

Located in Dun Glen, NV

Built in 1866 by James Hendra
- Gold miner and explorer
- Dun Glen NV founding father

Operated from 1866 to 1904

Processed over 1200 tons of material

Removed over $6 million in gold ($143 million today)

FIGURE A-18

HENDRA HOTEL HISTORY

James Hendra purchased the Dun Glen Hotel in 1873
- Originally built by William Chaffee in 1859
- Interior finished with custom milled knotty sugar pine from the Sierra Nevada
- Partially burned down in 1886 due to oil lamp fire in lobby

12 Hotel rooms
- Rooms rented for 25 cents a day or 2 dollars a week in 1873

Hendra died in 1910
- Hotel closed in 1911

Independent Challenge 1

You work for GTO Broadband Industries, a business that offers rural broadband Internet service and network server management. One of your jobs at the company is to present the company's services to local government and community meetings. Your boss has asked you to create a company profile presentation that describes the services GTO offers.

a. Start PowerPoint then open a new blank presentation.

b. In the title placeholder on Slide 1, type **GTO Broadband Industries**.

c. In the subtitle placeholder, type your name, press [Enter], then type today's date.

d. Apply the Slice design theme to the presentation.

e. Save your presentation with the filename **PPT A-Broadband** to the location where you store your Data Files.

f. Use **FIGURE A-19** and **FIGURE A-20** to add two more slides to your presentation. (*Hint*: Slide 2 uses the Comparison layout.)

g. Use the buttons on the VIEW tab to switch between all of PowerPoint's views.

h. Print the presentation using handouts, 3 Slides, in black and white.

i. Save and close the file, then exit PowerPoint.

FIGURE A-19

FIGURE A-20

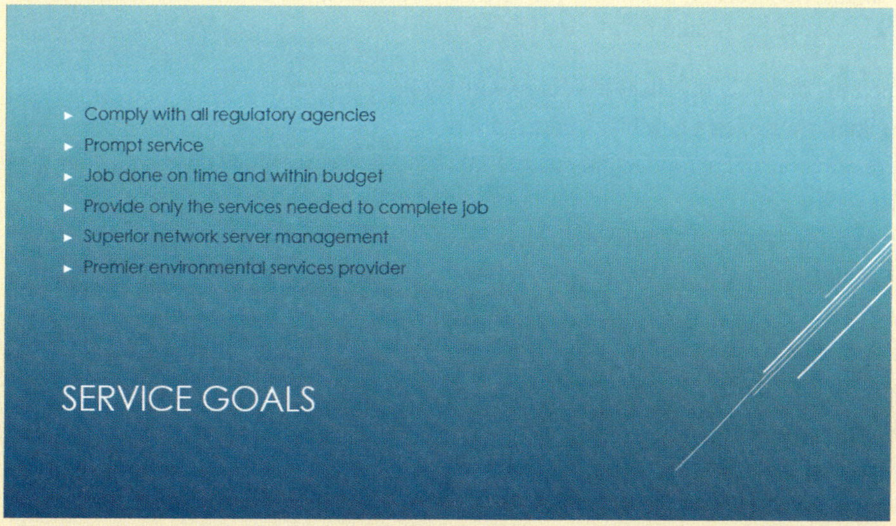

PowerPoint 2013

Independent Challenge 2

You have recently been promoted to sales manager at Goodrich Hardwood Industries, which sells and distributes specialty hardwood products used in flooring, cabinets, and furniture. Part of your job is to present company sales figures at a yearly sales meeting. Use the following information as the basis for units of wood sold nationally in your presentation: 425 units cherry, 260 units birch, 146 units hickory, 580 units mahogany, 345 units Brazilian walnut, 230 units American walnut, and 120 units pine. Assume that Goodrich Hardwood has five sales regions throughout the country: West, South, Midwest, Mid Atlantic, and Northeast. Also, assume the sales in each region rose between 1.5% and 4% over last year, and gross sales reached $67 million. The presentation should have at least five slides.

a. Spend some time planning the slides of your presentation. What is the best way to show the information provided? What other information could you add that might be useful for this presentation?

b. Start PowerPoint.

c. Give the presentation an appropriate title on the title slide, and enter today's date and your name in the subtitle placeholder.

d. Add slides and enter appropriate slide text.

e. On the last slide of the presentation, include the following information:
   Goodrich Hardwood Industries
   "Your specialty hardwood store"

f. Apply a design theme. A typical slide might look like the one shown in **FIGURE A-21**.

g. Switch views. Run through the slide show at least once.

h. Save your presentation with the filename **PPT A-Goodrich** where you store your Data Files.

i. Close the presentation and exit PowerPoint.

FIGURE A-21

TOTAL SALES BY UNIT

580 units – Mahogany
425 units – Cherry
345 units – Brazilian walnut
260 units – Birch
230 units – American walnut
146 units – Hickory
120 units – Pine

Independent Challenge 3

You work for Jamison Corporation, a company in Council Bluffs, Iowa, that is the primary international distributor of products made in Iowa. The marketing manager has asked you to plan and create a PowerPoint presentation that describes the products Iowa exports and the countries that import products made in Iowa. Describe Iowa's top exports, which include tractors, fresh and frozen pork meat, soybeans, corn, and aircraft engine parts. Also include information on top importers of Iowan products: Canada, Mexico, and Japan. Use the Internet, if possible, to research information that will help you formulate your ideas. The presentation should have at least five slides.

a. Spend some time planning the slides of your presentation.

b. Start PowerPoint then open a new blank presentation.

c. Give the presentation an appropriate title on the title slide, and enter today's date and your name in the subtitle placeholder.

d. Add slides and enter appropriate slide text.

e. On the last slide of the presentation, type the following information:
   Jamison Corp.
   Council Bluffs, Iowa
   Your Name

f. Apply a design theme.

g. Switch views. Run through the slide show at least once.

h. Save your presentation with the filename **PPT A-Jamison** to the location where you store your Data Files.

i. Close the presentation and exit PowerPoint.

Independent Challenge 4: Explore

You are a member of the Local Charity Society (LCS), a non-profit organization in Bellingham, Washington. It raises money throughout the year to support community needs such as schools, youth organizations, and other worthy causes. This year LCS has decided to support the Simpson Youth Center by hosting a regional barbeque cook-off, called the Master Pit-master Competition. The competition includes over 20 cooking teams from a five-state region. Create a presentation that describes the event.

a. Spend some time planning the slides of your presentation. Assume the following: the competition is a 2-day event; event advertising will be multistate wide; musical groups will be invited; there will events and games for kids; the event will be held at the county fairgrounds. Use the Internet, if possible, to research information that will help you formulate your ideas.

b. Start PowerPoint then open a new blank presentation.

c. Give the presentation an appropriate title on the title slide, and enter your name and today's date in the subtitle placeholder.

d. Add slides and enter appropriate slide text. You must create at least three slides.

e. Apply a Design Theme. Typical slides might look like the ones shown in **FIGURE A-22** and **FIGURE A-23**.

f. View the presentation.

g. Save your presentation with the filename **PPT A-Pitmaster** to the location where you store your Data Files.

h. Close the presentation and exit PowerPoint.

FIGURE A-22

JUDGING CATEGORIES

- Saturday – Prelims
  - 12:00pm – Brisket
  - 1:15pm – Chicken
  - 2:00pm - Sauces
  - 3:30pm – Pork
  - 4:15pm – Ribs
- Sunday – Finals
  - 12:00 am – Chicken
  - 12:30am – Sauces
  - 2:30pm – Brisket
  - 3:30pm – Ribs
  - 4:00pm - Pork
  - 4:45pm – Winner's Cook-off Round

FIGURE A-23

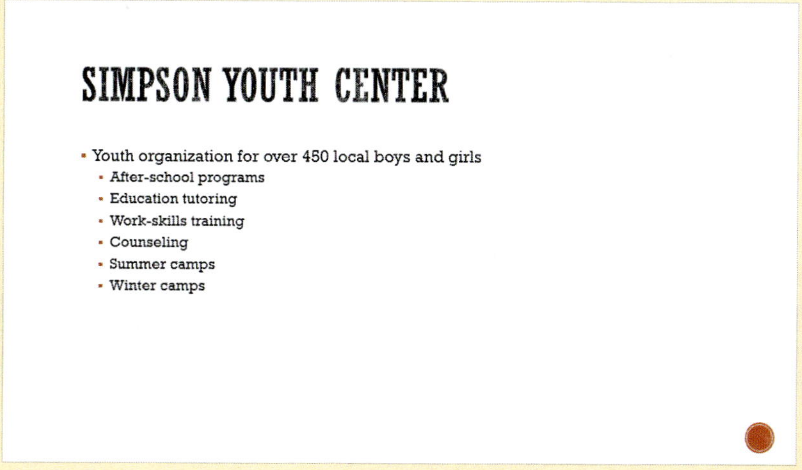

SIMPSON YOUTH CENTER

- Youth organization for over 450 local boys and girls
  - After-school programs
  - Education tutoring
  - Work-skills training
  - Counseling
  - Summer camps
  - Winter camps

Visual Workshop

Create the presentation shown in FIGURE A-24 and FIGURE A-25. Make sure you include your name on the title slide. Save the presentation as PPT A-LGS to the location where you store your Data Files. Print the slides.

FIGURE A-24

FIGURE A-25

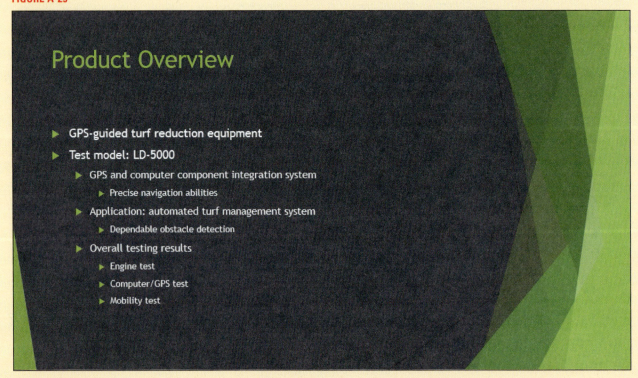

Modifying a Presentation

CASE You continue working on your Canadian Train tour presentation. In this unit, you'll enter text using Outline view, then you'll format text, create a SmartArt graphic, draw and modify objects, and add slide footer information in the presentation.

Unit Objectives

After completing this unit, you will be able to:

- Enter text in Outline view
- Format text
- Convert text to SmartArt
- Insert and modify shapes
- Rearrange and merge shapes
- Edit and duplicate shapes
- Align and group objects
- Add slide footers

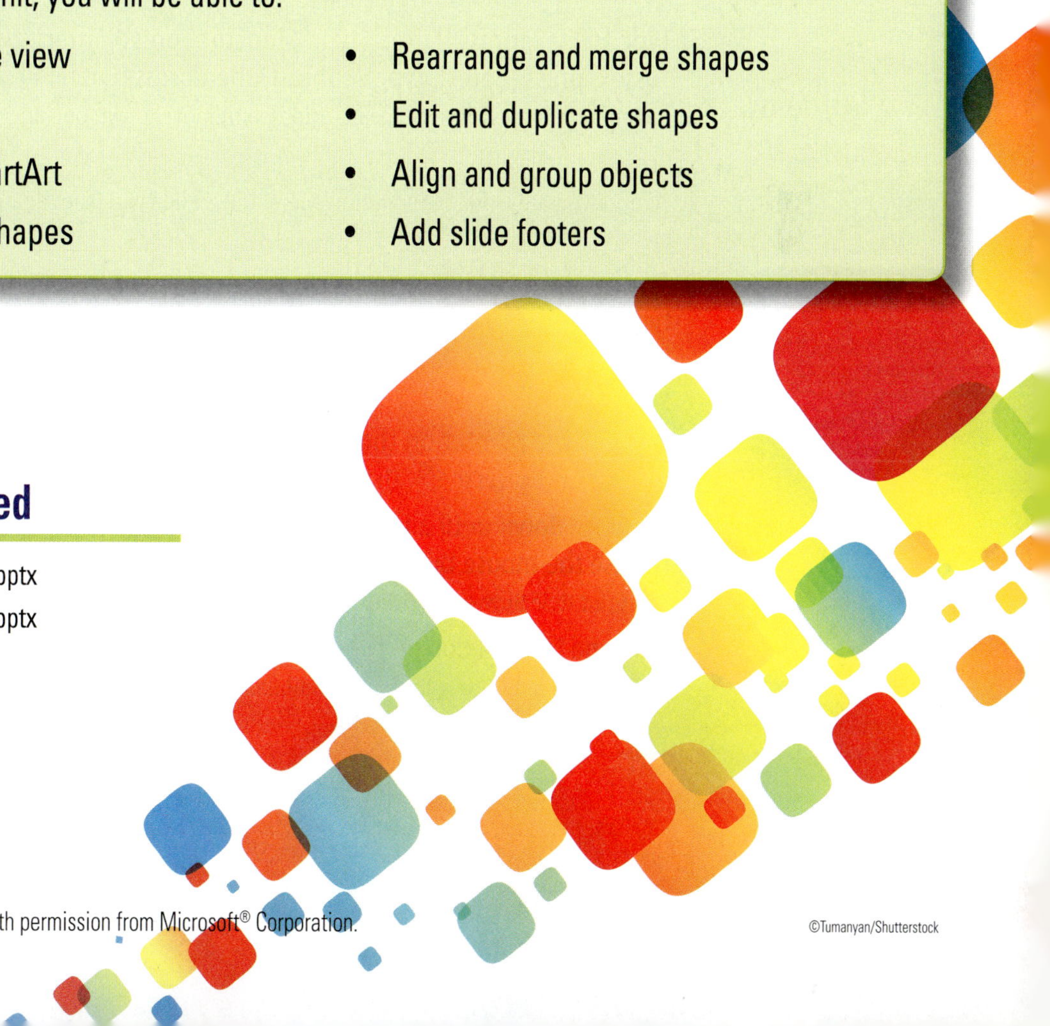

Files You Will Need

PPT B-1.pptx
PPT B-2.pptx
PPT B-3.pptx
PPT B-4.pptx
PPT B-5.pptx

©Tumanyan/Shutterstock

Enter Text in Outline View

Learning Outcomes
• Enter text in Outline view
• Create a new slide

You can enter presentation text by typing directly on the slide in the Slide pane, or, if you need to focus on the text of the presentation, you can enter text in Outline view. Text in Outline view is organized so the headings, or slide titles, appear at the top of the outline. Each subpoint, or each line of bulleted text, appears as one or more indented lines under the title. Each indent in the outline creates another level of bulleted text on the slide. **CASE** ▶ *You switch to Outline view to enter text for two more slides for your presentation.*

STEPS

1. **Start PowerPoint, open the presentation PPT B-1.pptx from the location where you store your Data Files, then save it as PPT B-QST.pptx**

   A presentation with the new name appears in the PowerPoint window.

2. **Click the Slide 2 thumbnail in the Thumbnails pane, click the New Slide button list arrow in the Slides group, then click Title and Content**

   A new slide, Slide 3, with the Title and Content layout appears as the current slide below Slide 2.

3. **Click the VIEW tab on the Ribbon, then click the Outline View button in the Presentation Views group**

   The text of the presentation appears in the Outline pane next to the Slide pane. The slide icon and the insertion point for Slide 3 are highlighted, indicating it is selected and ready to accept text. Text that you enter next to a slide icon becomes the title for that slide.

4. **Type Atlantic Region Stations, press [Enter], then press [Tab]**

   When you pressed [Enter] after typing the title, you created a new slide. However, because you want to enter bulleted text on Slide 3, you then pressed [Tab] so the text you type will be entered as bullet text on Slide 3. See **FIGURE B-1**.

5. **Type Halifax, press [Enter], type Moncton, press [Enter], type Gaspe, press [Enter], type Sussex, press [Enter], type Amherst, then press [Enter]**

   Each time you press [Enter], the insertion point moves down one line.

6. **Press [Shift][Tab]**

   Because you are working in Outline view, a new slide with the same layout, Slide 4, is created when you press [Shift][Tab].

7. **Type Atlantic Region Tour Packages, press [Ctrl][Enter], type Adventure, press [Enter], type Cultural, press [Enter], type Shopping, press [Enter], then type Wildlife**

   Pressing [Ctrl][Enter] while the insertion point is in the title text object moves the cursor into the content placeholder.

8. **Position the pointer on the Slide 3 icon ☐ in the Outline pane**

   The pointer changes to ✛. The Atlantic Region Stations slide, Slide 3, is out of order.

9. **Drag ☐ down until a horizontal indicator line appears above the Slide 5 icon, then release the mouse button**

   The third slide moves down and switches places with the fourth slide as shown in **FIGURE B-2**.

10. **Click the Normal button ▣ on the status bar, then save your work**

   The Outline pane closes, and the Thumbnails pane is now visible in the window.

FIGURE B-1: Outline view showing new slide

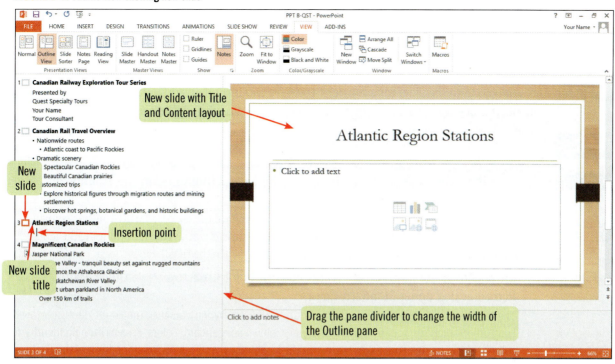

FIGURE B-2: Outline view showing moved slide

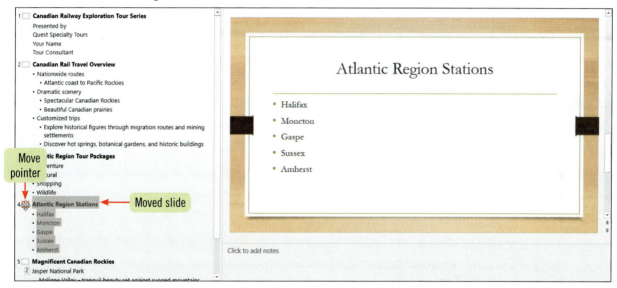

Using proofing tools for other languages

If you have a presentation in another language, how would you check the spelling and grammar of that presentation? Every version of PowerPoint contains a language pack with a primary language, such as English, Italian, or Arabic. Each language pack includes additional languages other than the primary language. For example, the English language pack also includes French and Spanish. So, let's say you have an English version of PowerPoint and you want to check the spelling of a presentation that is written in French. To check the spelling of a French presentation, click a text object on a slide, click the REVIEW tab on the Ribbon, click the Language button in the Language group, then click Set Proofing Language to open the Language dialog box. Click one of the French options from the list, then click OK. Only languages in the list with a spelling symbol are available to use for checking spelling and grammar. Now when you check the spelling, PowerPoint will do so in French. If your version of PowerPoint does not have the language you want to use, you can purchase additional language packs from Microsoft.

Format Text

Learning Outcomes
• Modify text characteristics

Once you have entered and edited the text in your presentation, you can modify the way the text looks to emphasize your message. Important text should be highlighted in some way to distinguish it from other text or objects on the slide. For example, if you have two text objects on the same slide, you could draw attention to one text object by changing its color, font, or size. **CASE** *You decide to format the text on Slide 2 of the presentation.*

STEPS

QUICK TIP

To show or hide the Mini toolbar, click the FILE tab on the Ribbon, click Options, then click the Show Mini Toolbar on selection check box.

1. **Click the HOME tab on the Ribbon, click the Slide 2 thumbnail in the Thumbnails pane, then double-click Rail in the title text object**

   The word "Rail" is selected, and a Mini toolbar appears above the text. The **Mini toolbar** contains basic text-formatting commands, such as bold and italic, and appears when you select text using the mouse. This toolbar makes it quick and easy to format text, especially when the HOME tab is closed.

2. **Move ⬐ over the Mini toolbar, click the Font Color list arrow 🅰 ⁃, then click the Dark Red color box under Standard Colors**

   The text changes color to dark red as shown in **FIGURE B-3**. When you click the Font Color list arrow, the Font Color gallery appears showing the Theme Colors and Standard Colors. ScreenTips help identify font colors. Notice that the Font Color button on the Mini toolbar and the Font Color button in the Font group on the HOME tab change color to reflect the new color choice, which is now the active color.

QUICK TIP

To select an unselected text object, press [Shift], click the text object, then release [Shift].

3. **Move the pointer over the title text object border until the pointer changes to ⬐, then click the border**

   The border changes from a dashed to a solid line as you move the pointer over the text object border. The entire title text object is selected, and changes you make now affect all of the text in the text object. When the whole text object is selected, you can change its size, shape, and other attributes. Changing the color of the text helps emphasize it.

QUICK TIP

For more text formatting options, right-click a text object, then click Format Text Effects to open the Format Shape - Text Options pane.

4. **Click the Font Color button 🅰 in the Font group**

   All of the text in the title text object changes to the current active color, dark red.

5. **Click the Font list arrow in the Font group**

   A list of available fonts opens with Garamond, the current font used in the title text object, selected at the top of the list in the Theme Fonts section.

6. **Scroll down the alphabetical list, then click Castellar in the All Fonts section**

   The Castellar font replaces the original font in the title text object. Notice that as you move the pointer over the font names in the font list the text on the slide displays a Live Preview of the different font choices.

7. **Click the Underline button 🅄 in the Font group, then click the Increase Font Size button 🅰 in the Font group**

   All of the text now displays an underline and increases in size to 44.

8. **Click the Character Spacing button 🔤 ⁃ in the Font group, then click Very Loose**

   The spacing between the letters in the title increases. Compare your screen to **FIGURE B-4**.

9. **Click a blank area of the slide outside the text object to deselect it, then save your work**

   Clicking a blank area of the slide deselects all objects that are selected.

FIGURE B-3: Selected word with Mini toolbar open

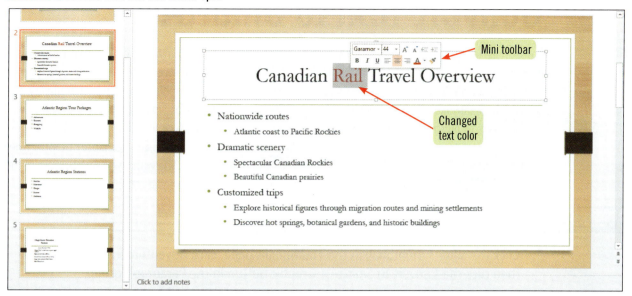

FIGURE B-4: Formatted text

Replacing text and fonts

As you review your presentation, you may decide to replace certain text or fonts throughout the entire presentation using the Replace command. Text can be a word, phrase, or sentence. To replace specific text, click the HOME tab on the Ribbon, then click the Replace button in the Editing group. In the Replace dialog box, enter the text you want to replace, then enter the text you want to use as its replacement. You can also use the Replace command to replace one font for another. Simply click the Replace button list arrow in the Editing group, then click Replace Fonts to open the Replace Font dialog box.

Convert Text to SmartArt

Sometimes when you are working with text it just doesn't capture your attention, no matter how you dress it up with color or other formatting attributes. The ability to convert text to a SmartArt graphic increases your ability to create dynamic-looking text. A **SmartArt** graphic is a professional-quality diagram that visually illustrates text. There are eight categories, or types, of SmartArt graphics that incorporate graphics to illustrate text differently. For example, you can show steps in a process or timeline, show proportional relationships, or show how parts relate to a whole. You can create a SmartArt graphic from scratch or create one by converting existing text you have entered on a slide with a few simple clicks of the mouse. **CASE** *You want the presentation to appear visually dynamic so you convert the text on Slide 3 to a SmartArt graphic.*

STEPS

1. **Click the Slide 3 thumbnail in the Thumbnails pane, click Adventure in the text object, then click the Convert to SmartArt Graphic button in the Paragraph group**

   A gallery of SmartArt graphic layouts opens. As with many features in PowerPoint, you can preview how your text will look prior to applying the SmartArt graphic layout by using PowerPoint's Live Preview feature. You can review each SmartArt graphic layout and see how it changes the appearance of the text.

2. **Move ⬚ over the SmartArt graphic layouts in the gallery**

   Notice how the text becomes part of the graphic and the color and font changes each time you move the pointer over a different graphic layout. SmartArt graphic names appear in ScreenTips.

3. **Click the Vertical Picture Accent List layout in the SmartArt graphics gallery**

   A SmartArt graphic appears on the slide in place of the text object, and a new SMARTART TOOLS DESIGN tab opens on the Ribbon as shown in **FIGURE B-5**. A SmartArt graphic consists of two parts: the SmartArt graphic itself and a Text pane where you type and edit text. This graphic also has placeholders where you can add pictures to the SmartArt graphic.

4. **Click each bullet point in the Text pane, then click the Text pane control button ⬚**

   Notice that each time you select a bullet point in the text pane, a selection box appears around the text objects in the SmartArt graphic. The Text pane control opens and closes the Text pane. You can also open and close the Text pane using the Text Pane button in the Create Graphic group.

5. **Click the More button ⬚ in the Layouts group, click More Layouts to open the Choose a SmartArt Graphic dialog box, click Relationship, click the Basic Venn layout icon, then click OK**

   The SmartArt graphic changes to the new graphic layout. You can radically change how the SmartArt graphic looks by applying a SmartArt Style. A **SmartArt Style** is a preset combination of simple and 3-D formatting options that follows the presentation theme.

6. **Move ⬚ slowly over the styles in the SmartArt Styles group, then click the More button ⬚ in the SmartArt Styles group**

   A Live Preview of each style is displayed on the SmartArt graphic. The SmartArt styles are organized into sections; the top group offers suggestions for the best match for the document, and the bottom group shows you all of the possible 3-D styles that are available.

7. **Move ⬚ over the styles in the gallery, then click Cartoon in the 3-D section**

   Notice how this new style adds a black outline and shading to each object to achieve the 3-D effect.

8. **Click a blank area of the slide outside the SmartArt graphic object to deselect it, then save your work**

   Compare your screen to **FIGURE B-6**.

Modifying a Presentation

FIGURE B-5: Text converted to a SmartArt graphic

FIGURE B-6: Final SmartArt graphic

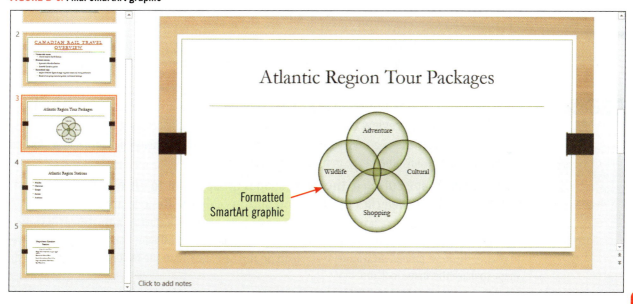

Choosing SmartArt graphics

When choosing a SmartArt graphic to use on your slide, remember that you want the SmartArt graphic to communicate the message of the text effectively; not every SmartArt graphic layout achieves that goal. You must consider the type of text you want to illustrate. For example, does the text show steps in a process, does it show a continual process, or does it show nonsequential information? The answer to this question will dictate the type of SmartArt graphic layout you should choose. Also, the amount of text you want to illustrate will have an effect on the SmartArt graphic layout you choose. Most of the time key points will be the text you use in a SmartArt graphic. Finally, some SmartArt graphic layouts are limited by the number of shapes they can accommodate, so be sure to choose a graphic layout that can illustrate your text appropriately. Experiment with the SmartArt graphic layouts until you find the right one, and have fun in the process!

Insert and Modify Shapes

Learning Outcomes
• Create a shape
• Modify a shape's style

In PowerPoint you can insert many different types of shapes including lines, geometric figures, arrows, stars, callouts, and banners to enhance your presentation. You can modify many aspects of a shape including its fill color, line color, and line style, as well as add other effects like shadow and 3-D effects. Another way to alter the way a shape looks is to apply a Quick Style. A **Quick Style** is a set of formatting options, including line style, fill color, and effects. **CASE** ▸ *You decide to draw some shapes on Slide 4 of your presentation that identify the Atlantic regional train stations.*

STEPS

1. **Click the Slide 4 thumbnail in the Thumbnails pane, click the Oval button ◯ in the Drawing group, then position ✛ in the blank area of the slide below the slide title**
   Slide 4 appears in the Slide pane. ScreenTips help you identify the shapes.

2. **Press and hold [Shift], drag ✛ down and to the right to create the shape, as shown in FIGURE B-7, release the mouse button, then release [Shift]**
   A circle shape appears on the slide, filled with the default theme color. Pressing [Shift] while you create the object maintains the object proportions as you change its size, so you create a circle using the oval tool. A **rotate handle**—small round arrow—appears on top of the shape, which you can drag to manually rotate the shape. To change the style of the shape, apply a Quick Style from the Shape Styles group.

3. **Click the DRAWING TOOLS FORMAT tab on the Ribbon, click the More button ▾ in the Shape Styles group, move ⌕ over the styles in the gallery to review the effects on the shape, then click Subtle Effect - Blue-Grey, Accent 3**
   A blue Quick Style with coordinated gradient fill, line, and shadow color is applied to the shape.

4. **Click the Shape Outline list arrow in the Shape Styles group, point to Weight, move ⌕ over the line weight options to review the effect on the shape, then click 3 pt**
   The outline weight (or width) increases and is easier to see now.

5. **Click the Shape Effects button in the Shape Styles group, point to Preset, move ⌕ over the effect options to review the effect on the shape, then click Preset 3**
   Lighting and shadow effects are added to the shape to give it a three-dimensional appearance. You can change the shape to any other shape in the shapes gallery.

6. **Click the Edit Shape button in the Insert Shapes group, point to Change Shape to open the shapes gallery, then click the Teardrop button ◯ in the Basic Shapes section**
   The circle shape changes to a teardrop shape and a new yellow handle—called an **adjustment handle**—appears in the upper-right corner of the shape. Some shapes have an adjustment handle that can be moved to change the most prominent feature of an object, in this case the end of the teardrop. You can rotate the shape to make the shape look different.

7. **Click the Rotate button in the Arrange group, move ⌕ over the rotation options to review the effect on the shape, then click Flip Vertical**
   Notice that the rotate handle is now on the bottom of the shape indicating that the shape has flipped vertically, or rotated 180 degrees, as shown in **FIGURE B-8**. You prefer the circle shape, and you decide the shape looks better rotated back the way it was before.

8. **Click the Undo button list arrow ↺ ▾ in the Quick Access Toolbar, click Change Shape, click a blank area of the slide, then save your work**
   The last two commands you performed are undone, and the shape changes back to a circle and is flipped back to its original position. Clicking a blank area of the slide deselects all objects that are selected.

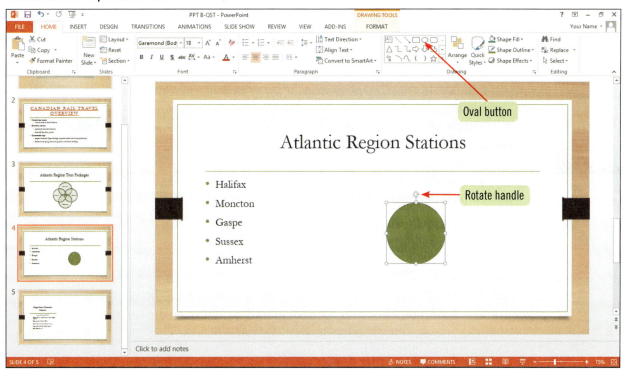

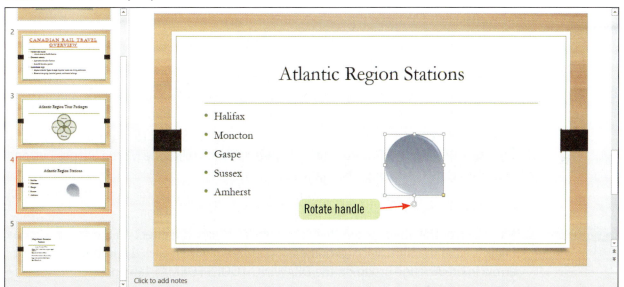

Use the Eyedropper to match colors

As you develop your presentation and work with different shapes and pictures, sometimes from other sources, there may be a certain color that is not in the theme colors of the presentation that you want to capture and apply to objects in your presentation. To capture a color on a specific slide, select any object on the slide, click any button list arrow with a color feature, such as the Shape Fill button or the Shape Outline button on the DRAWING TOOLS FORMAT tab, then click Eyedropper. Move the over the color you want to capture and pause, or hover. As you hover over a color, a Live Preview of the color appears and the RGB (Red Green Blue) values, called coordinates, appear in a ScreenTip. Click when you see the color you want to capture. The new color now appears in any color gallery under Recent Colors. If you decide not to capture a new color, press [Esc] to close the Eyedropper without making any change.

Rearrange and Merge Shapes

Every object on a slide, whether it is a shape, a picture, a text object, or any other object, is placed, or stacked, on the slide in the order it was created, like pieces of paper placed one on top of another. Each object on a slide can be moved up or down in the stack depending how you want the objects to look on the slide. **Merging** shapes, which combines multiple shapes together, provides you the potential to create a variety of unique geometric shapes that are not available in the Shapes gallery. **CASE** ➤ *You create a diamond shape on Slide 4 and then merge it with the circle shape.*

STEPS

1. **Click Gaspe in the text object, position ⬚ over the right-middle sizing handle, ⬚ changes to ⬚, then drag the sizing handle to the left until the right border of the text object is under the first word in the title text object**

   The width of the text object decreases. When you position ⬚ over a sizing handle, it changes to ⬚. This pointer points in different directions depending on which sizing handle it is over.

2. **Click the More button ⬚ in the Drawing group, click the Diamond button ◇ in the Basic Shapes section, then drag down and to the right to create the shape**

   Compare your screen to FIGURE B-9. A diamond shape appears on the slide, filled with the default theme color. You can move shapes by dragging them on the slide.

3. **Drag the diamond shape over the circle shape, then use the Smart Guides that appear to position the diamond shape in the center of the circle shape where the guides intersect**

   Smart Guides, help you position objects relative to each other and determine equal distances between objects.

4. **Click the Select button in the Editing group, click Selection Pane, then click the Send Backward button ⬚ in the Selection pane once**

   The Selection pane opens on the right side of the window showing the four objects on the slide and the order they are stacked on the slide. The Send Backward and Bring Forward buttons let you change the stacking order. The diamond shape moves back one position in the stack behind the circle shape.

5. **Press [SHIFT], click the circle shape on the slide, release [SHIFT] to select both shapes, click the DRAWING TOOLS FORMAT tab on the Ribbon, click the Merge Shapes button in the Insert Shapes group, then point to Union**

   The two shapes appear to merge, or combine, together to form one shape. The merged shape assumes the theme and formatting style of the diamond shape because it was selected first.

6. **Move ⬚ over the other merge shapes options to review the effect on the shape, click a blank area of the slide twice, click the diamond shape, then click the Bring Forward list arrow in the Arrange group on the DRAWING TOOLS FORMAT tab once**

   Each merge option produces a different result. The diamond shape moves back to the top of the stack. Now, you want to see what happens when you select the circle shape first before you merge the two shapes together.

7. **Click the circle shape, press [SHIFT], click the diamond shape, click the Merge Shapes button in the Insert Shapes group, then point to Union**

   The merged shape adopts the theme and formatting style of the circle shape.

8. **Point to each of the merge shapes options, then click Subtract**

   The two shapes merge into one shape. This merge option deletes the area of all shapes from the first shape you selected, so in this case the area of the diamond shape is deleted from the circle shape. The merged shape is identified as Freeform 6 in the Selection pane. See FIGURE B-10.

9. **Click the Selection Pane button in the Arrange group, click a blank area of the slide, then save your work**

Modifying a Presentation

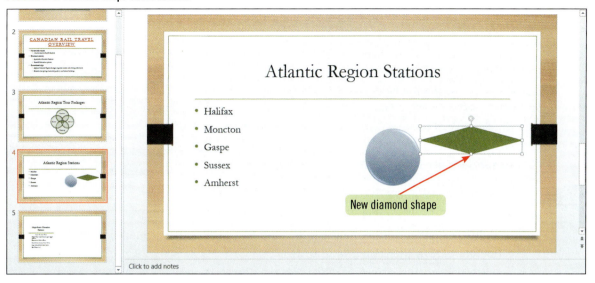

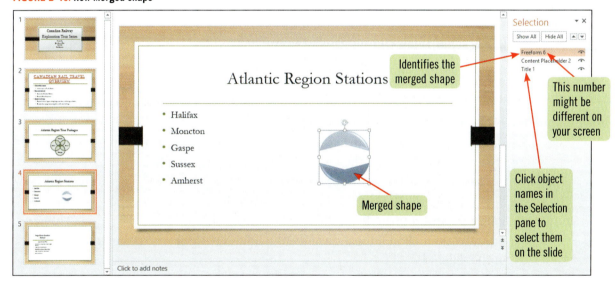

Changing the size and position of shapes

Usually when you resize a shape you can simply drag one of the sizing handles around the outside of the shape, but some-times you may need to resize a shape more precisely. When you select a shape, the DRAWING TOOLS FORMAT tab appears on the Ribbon, offering you many different formatting options including some sizing commands located in the Size group.

The Width and Height commands in the Size group allow you to change the width and height of a shape. You also have the option to open the Format Shape pane, which allows you to change the size of a shape, as well as the rotation, scale, and position of a shape on the slide.

Edit and Duplicate Shapes

Once you have created a shape you still have the ability to refine its basic characteristics, which helps change the size and appearance of the shape. For example, if you create a shape and it is too large, you can reduce its size by dragging any of its sizing handles. Most PowerPoint shapes can have text attached to them. All shapes can be moved and copied. To help you resize and move shapes and other objects precisely, PowerPoint has rulers you can add to the Slide pane. Rulers display the measurement system your computer uses, either inches or metric measurements. **CASE** *You want three identical circle shapes on Slide 4. You first add the ruler to the slide to help you change the size of the circle shape you've already created, and then you make copies of it.*

STEPS

1. **Right-click a blank area of Slide 4, click Ruler on the shortcut menu, then click the bottom part of the circle shape to select it**

   Rulers appear on the left and top of the Slide pane. Unless the ruler has been changed to metric measurements, it is divided into inches and half-inch and eighth-inch marks. Notice the current location of the ꝅ is identified on both rulers by a small dotted red line in the ruler.

2. **Press [Shift], drag the lower-right sizing handle on the circle shape up and to the left approximately 1/4", release the mouse button, then release [Shift]**

   The distance of a quarter-inch on the ruler is the distance between two lines. The circle shape is now slightly smaller in diameter.

3. **Position ꝅ over the selected circle shape so it changes to ꝅ, then drag the circle shape to the Smart Guides on the slide as shown in FIGURE B-11**

   PowerPoint uses a series of evenly spaced horizontal and vertical lines—called **gridlines**—to align objects, which force objects to "snap" to the grid.

4. **Position ꝅ over the bottom part of the circle shape, then press and hold [Ctrl]**

   The pointer changes to ꝅ, indicating that PowerPoint makes a copy of the shape when you drag the mouse.

5. **Holding [Ctrl], drag the circle shape to the right until the circle shape copy is in a blank area of the slide, release the mouse button, then release [Ctrl]**

   An identical copy of the circle shape appears on the slide and Smart Guides appear above and below the shape as you drag the new shape to the right, which helps you align the shapes.

6. **With the second circle shape still selected, click the Copy list arrow in the Clipboard group, click Duplicate, then move the duplicated circle shape to the right in a blank area of the slide**

   You have duplicated the circle shape twice and now have three shapes on the slide.

7. **Click the VIEW tab on the Ribbon, click the Ruler check box in the Show group, click the HOME tab, then type Excursions**

   The ruler closes, and the text you type appears in the selected circle shape and becomes a part of the shape. Now if you move or rotate the shape, the text moves with it. Compare your screen with FIGURE B-12.

8. **Click the middle circle shape, type Getaways, click the left circle shape, type Holidays, click in a blank area of the slide, then save your work**

   All three circle shapes include text.

Modifying a Presentation

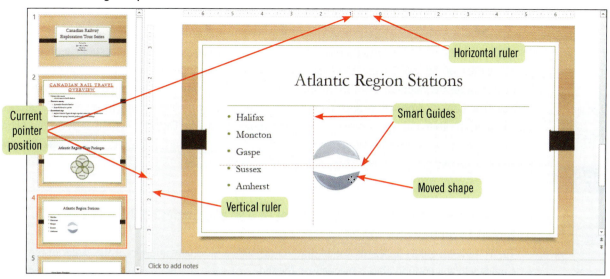

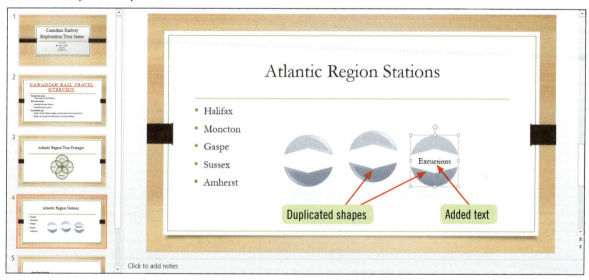

Editing points of a shape

If you want to customize the form (or outline) of any shape in the shapes gallery, you can modify its edit points. To display a shape's edit points, select the shape you want to modify, click the DRAWING TOOLS FORMAT tab on the Ribbon, click the Edit Shape button in the Insert Shapes group, then click Edit Points. Black edit points appear on the shape. To change the form of a shape, drag a black edit point. When you click a black edit point white square edit points appear on either side of the black edit point, which allow you to change the curvature of a line between two black edit points. When you are finished with your custom shape, you can save it as picture and reuse it in other presentations or other files. To save the shape as a picture, right-click the shape, then click Save as Picture.

Align and Group Objects

Learning Outcomes
• Move shapes using guides
• Align and group shapes
• Distribute shapes

After you are finished creating and modifying your objects, you can position them accurately on the slide to achieve the look you want. Using the Align commands in the Arrange group, you can align objects relative to each other by snapping them to the gridlines on a slide or to guides that you manually position on the slide. The Group command groups two or more objects into one object, which secures their relative position to each other and makes it easy to edit and move them. The Distribute commands on the Align list evenly space objects horizontally or vertically relative to each other or the slide. **CASE** ▶ *You are ready to position and group the circle shapes on Slide 4 to finish the slide.*

STEPS

1. **Right-click a blank area of the slide, point to Grid and Guides on the shortcut menu, then click Guides**

   The PowerPoint guides appear as dotted lines on the slide and usually intersect at the center of the slide. Guides help you position objects precisely on the slide.

2. **Position � over the horizontal guide in a blank area of the slide, notice the pointer change to ☰, press and hold the mouse button until the pointer changes to a measurement guide box, then drag the guide up until the guide position box reads .42**

QUICK TIP
To set the formatting of a shape as the default, right-click the shape, then click Set as Default Shape on the Shortcut menu.

3. **Drag the vertical guide to the left until the guide position box reads 2.92, then drag the Holidays circle shape so the top and left edges of the shape touch the guides as shown in FIGURE B-13**

   The Holidays circle shape attaches or "snaps" to the guides.

4. **Drag the Excursions circle shape to the right until it touches a vertical Smart Guide, press and hold [Shift], click the other two circle shapes, then release [Shift]**

   All three shapes are now selected.

5. **Click the DRAWING TOOLS FORMAT tab on the Ribbon, click the Align button in the Arrange group, click Align Top, then click a blank area of the slide**

   The lower shapes move up and align with the top shape along their top edges. The right circle shape would look better if it were lined up with the line under the title.

6. **Drag the vertical guide to the right until the guide position box reads 5.17, then drag the Excursions circle shape to the left so the top and right edges of the shape touch the guides**

   The Excursions circle shape moves to the left and is now lined up with a design element on the slide.

QUICK TIP
To quickly add a new guide to the slide, press [Ctrl], then drag an existing guide. The original guide remains in place. Drag a guide off the slide to delete it.

7. **Press and hold [Shift], click the other two circle shapes, release [Shift], click the DRAWING TOOLS FORMAT tab, then click the Align button in the Arrange group**

8. **Click Distribute Horizontally, click the Group button in the Arrange group, then click Group**

   The shapes are now distributed equally between themselves and grouped together to form one object without losing their individual attributes, as shown in FIGURE B-14. Notice that the sizing handles and rotate handle now appear on the outer edge of the grouped object, not around each individual object.

9. **Drag the horizontal guide to the middle of the slide until its guide position box reads 0.00, then drag the vertical guide to the middle of the slide until its guide position box reads 0.00**

10. **Click the VIEW tab on the Ribbon, click the Guides check box in the Show group, click a blank area of the slide, then save your work**

    The guides are no longer displayed on the slide

FIGURE B-13: Repositioned shape

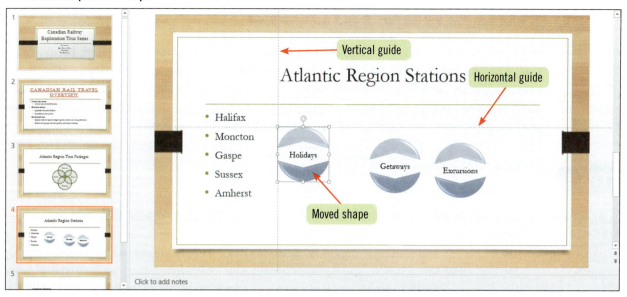

FIGURE B-14: Aligned and grouped shapes

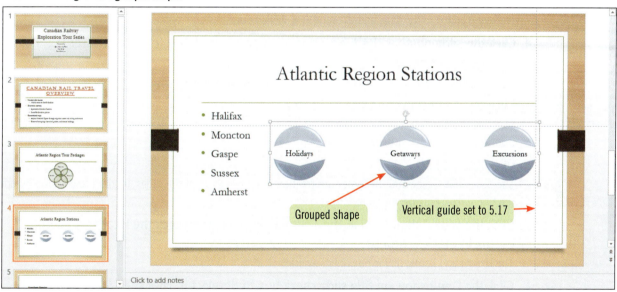

Distributing objects

There are two ways to distribute objects in PowerPoint: relative to each other and relative to the slide edge. If you choose to distribute objects relative to each other, PowerPoint evenly divides the empty space between all of the selected objects. When distributing objects in relation to the slide, PowerPoint evenly splits the empty space from slide edge to slide edge between the selected objects. To distribute objects relative to each other, click the Align button in the Arrange group on the DRAWING TOOLS FORMAT tab, then click Align Selected Objects. To distribute objects relative to the slide, click the Align button in the Arrange group on the DRAWING TOOLS FORMAT tab, then click Align to Slide.

Add Slide Footers

Learning Outcomes
• Add footer text to slides

Footer text, such as a company, school, or product name, the slide number, or the date, can give your slides a professional look and make it easier for your audience to follow your presentation. Slides do not have headers but can include a footer; however, notes or handouts can include both header and footer text. You can review footer information that you apply to the slides in the PowerPoint views and when you print the slides. Notes and handouts header and footer text is visible when you print notes pages, handouts, and the outline. **CASE** ▶ *You add footer text to the slides of the Canadian train tour presentation to make it easier for the audience to follow.*

STEPS

QUICK TIP
The placement of the footer text objects on the slide is dependent on the presentation theme.

1. **Click the INSERT tab on the Ribbon, then click the Header & Footer button in the Text group**
   The Header and Footer dialog box opens, as shown in **FIGURE B-15**. The Header and Footer dialog box has two tabs: a Slide tab and a Notes and Handouts tab. The Slide tab is selected. There are three types of footer text, Date and time, Slide number, and Footer. The rectangles at the bottom of the Preview box identify the default position and status of the three types of footer text placeholders on the slides.

2. **Click the Date and time check box to select it**
   The date and time options are now available to select. The Update automatically date and time option button is selected by default. This option updates the date and time every time you open or print the file.

QUICK TIP
If you want a specific date to appear every time you view or print the presentation, click the Fixed date option button, then type the date in the Fixed text box.

3. **Click the Update automatically list arrow, then click the second option in the list**
   The day is added to the date, and the month is spelled out.

4. **Click the Slide number check box, click the Footer check box, click the Footer text box, then type your name**
   The Preview box now shows all three footer placeholders are selected.

5. **Click the Don't show on title slide check box**
   Selecting this check box prevents the footer information you entered in the Header and Footer dialog box from appearing on the title slide.

6. **Click Apply to All**
   The dialog box closes, and the footer information is applied to all of the slides in your presentation except the title slide. Compare your screen to **FIGURE B-16**.

7. **Click the Slide 1 thumbnail in the Thumbnails pane, then click the Header & Footer button in the Text group**
   The Header and Footer dialog box opens again.

8. **Click the Don't show on title slide check box to deselect it, click the Footer check box, then select the text in the Footer text box**

TROUBLE
If you click Apply to All in Step 9, click the Undo button on the Quick Access toolbar and repeat Steps 7, 8, and 9.

9. **Type Once in a lifetime travel experiences, click Apply, then save your work**
   Only the text in the Footer text box appears on the title slide. Clicking Apply applies the footer information to just the current slide.

10. **Submit your presentation to your instructor, then exit PowerPoint**

FIGURE B-15: Header and Footer dialog box

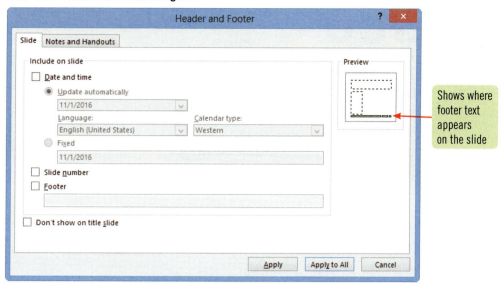

FIGURE B-16: Footer information added to presentation

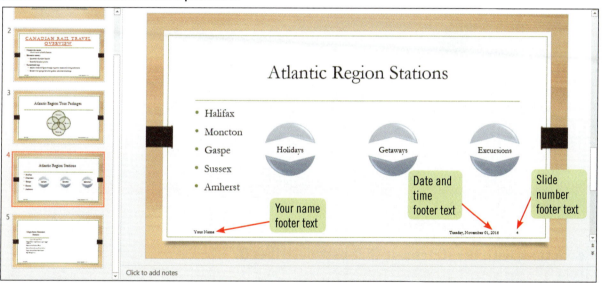

Creating superscript and subscript text

Superscript or subscript text is a number, figure, symbol, or letters that appears smaller than other text and is positioned above or below the normal line of text. A common superscript in the English language is the sign indicator next to number, such as, 1st or 3rd. Other examples of superscripts are the trademark symbol™ and the copyright symbol©. To create superscript text in PowerPoint, select the text, number, or symbol, then press [CTRL] [SHIFT] [+] at the same time. Probably the most familiar subscript text are the numerals in chemical compounds and formulas, for example, H_2O and CO_2. To create subscript text, select the text, number, or symbol, then press [CTRL] [=] at the same time. To change superscript or subscript text back to normal text, select the text, then press [CTRL] [Spacebar].

Practice

Concepts Review

Label each element of the PowerPoint window shown in FIGURE B-17.

FIGURE B-17

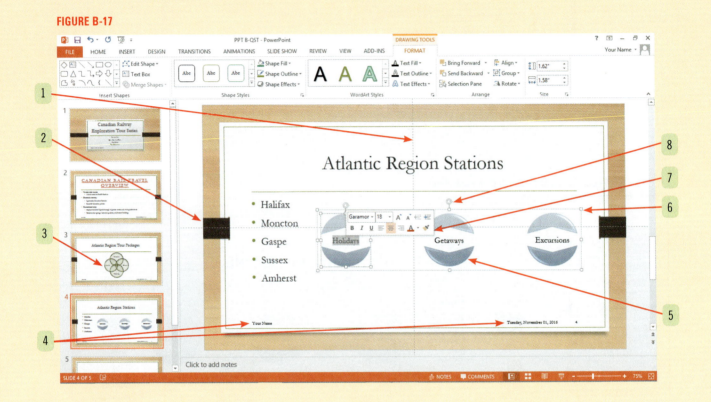

Match each term with the statement that best describes it.

9. **SmartArt graphic**
10. **Merge**
11. **Adjustment handle**
12. **Smart Guides**
13. **Quick Style**
14. **Rotate handle**

a. A diagram that visually illustrates text
b. A preset combination of formatting options you apply to an object
c. Combines multiple shapes together into one shape
d. Yellow handle that changes the most prominent feature of an object
e. Short red dashed lines that appear on the slide
f. Use to drag to turn an object

Select the best answer from the list of choices.

15. What appears just above text when it is selected?
a. AutoFit Options button
b. Mini toolbar
c. QuickStyles
d. Option button

16. Which of the following statements is *not* true about Outline view?
a. It is organized using headings and subpoints.
b. Pressing [Enter] moves the insertion point down one line.
c. Each line of indented text creates a new slide title.
d. Headings are the same as slide titles.

17. Why would you use the Eyedropper tool?
a. To save a 3-D effect for future use
b. To pick up font styles from a text object
c. To soften the edges of a shape
d. To add a new color to the color gallery

18. Which of the following statements about merged shapes is *not* true?
a. A merged shape is a combination of multiple shapes.
b. Merged shapes are unique geometric shapes found in the shapes gallery.
c. A merged shape assumes the theme of the shape that is selected first.
d. The stacking order of shapes changes the way a merged shape looks.

19. A professional-quality diagram that visually illustrates text best describes which of the following?
a. A SmartArt graphic
b. A SmartArt Style
c. A merged shape
d. A subscript

20. What do objects snap to when you move them?
a. Shape edges
b. Anchor points
c. Gridlines
d. Slide edges

21. What is *not* true about grouped objects?
a. Each object is distributed relative to the slide edges.
b. Grouped objects have one rotate handle.
c. Grouped objects act as one object but maintain their individual attributes.
d. Sizing handles appear around the grouped object.

Skills Review

FIGURE B-18

1. Enter text in Outline view.
a. Open the presentation PPT B-2.
   pptx from the location where you
   store your Data Files, then save it
   as **PPT B-ProPool**. The completed presentation is shown in
   FIGURE B-18.
b. Create a new slide after Slide 2
   with the Title and Content layout.
c. Open Outline view, then type
   Use and Application.
d. Press [Enter], press [Tab], type
   City water utilities, press
   [Enter], type **State water
   districts**, press [Enter], type
   Private water sources, press [Enter], then type **Commercial pools**.

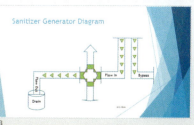

Skills Review (continued)

  e. Move Slide 3 below Slide 4, then, switch back to Normal view.

  f. Click the HOME tab, then save your changes.

2. Format text.

  a. Go to Slide 1.

  b. Select the name R.J. Palmer, then move the pointer over the Mini toolbar.

  c. Click the Font Color list arrow, then click Red under Standard Colors.

  d. Select the text object, then change all of the text to the color Red.

  e. Click the Font Size list arrow, then click 24.

  f. Click the Italic button.

  g. Click the Character Spacing button, then click Very Tight.

  h. Save your changes.

3. Convert text to SmartArt.

  a. Click the text object on Slide 4.

  b. Click the Convert to SmartArt Graphic button, then apply the Basic Cycle graphic layout to the text object.

  c. Click the More button in the Layouts group, click More Layouts, click Matrix in the Choose a SmartArt Graphic dialog box, click Grid Matrix, then click OK.

  d. Click the More button in the SmartArt Styles group, then apply the Moderate Effect style from the Best Match for Document group to the graphic.

  e. Close the text pane if necessary, then click outside the SmartArt graphic in a blank part of the slide.

  f. Save your changes.

4. Insert and modify shapes.

  a. Go to Slide 3, then add rulers to the Slide pane.

  b. Click the More button in the Drawing group to open the Shapes gallery, click the Plus button in the Equation Shapes section, press [Shift], then draw a two inch shape in a blank area of the slide.

  c. On the DRAWING TOOLS FORMAT tab, click the More button in the Shape Styles group, then click Colored Fill – Green, Accent 6.

  d. Click the Shape Effects button, point to Shadow, then click Offset Diagonal Bottom Right.

FIGURE B-19

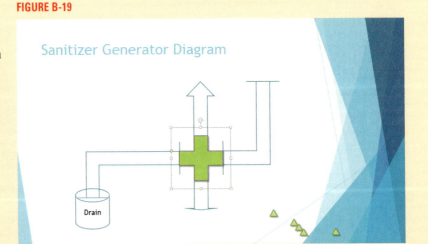

  e. Click the Shape Outline list arrow, then click Black, Text 1, Lighter 50% in the Theme Colors section.

  f. Drag the Plus shape to the small open area in the middle of the diagram, adjust the shape if needed to make it fit in the space as shown in FIGURE B-19, then save your changes.

5. Rearrange and merge shapes.

  a. Click the title text object on Slide 3, then drag the bottom-middle sizing handle up to fit the text in the text object.

  b. Click the More button in the Insert Shapes group, click the Hexagon button in the Basic Shapes section, press and hold [Shift], then draw a 1-inch shape.

  c. Drag the hexagon shape over top of the plus shape and center it, then open the Selection pane.

  d. Send the hexagon shape back one level, press [Shift], click the plus shape, then click the Merge Shapes button in the Insert Shapes group on the DRAWING TOOLS FORMAT tab.

Skills Review (continued)

e. Point to each of the merge shapes options, click a blank area of the slide twice, then click the plus shape.

f. Send the plus shape back one level, press [Shift], click the hexagon shape, click the Merge Shapes button, then click Combine.

g. Close the Selection pane, then save your work.

6. **Edit and duplicate shapes.**

a. Select the up-angled shape to the right of the merged shape, then using [Ctrl] make one copy of the shape.

b. Use Smart Guides to align the new up-angled shape just to the right of the original shape.

c. Click the Rotate button in the Arrange group, click Flip Vertical, click the Undo button, click the Rotate button, then click Flip Horizontal.

d. Type **Bypass**, click the up-angled shape to the right of the merged shape, type **Flow In**, click the down-angled shape to the left of the merged shape, then type **Flow Out**.

e. Click the arrow shape above the merged shape, then drag the top-middle sizing handle down 1/2 inch.

f. Click a blank area of the slide, add the guides to the Slide pane, then save your changes.

7. **Align and group objects.**

a. Move the vertical guide to the left until 3.83 appears, drag a selection box to select the five small green triangle shapes at the bottom of the slide, then click the DRAWING TOOLS FORMAT tab.

b. Click the Align button in the Arrange group, click Align Middle, click the Align button, then click Distribute Horizontally.

c. Click the Rotate button in the Arrange group, click Rotate Left 90°, click the Group button in the Arrange group, then click Group.

d. Move the grouped triangle shape object to the guide in the blank space on the down-angled shape to the left of the merged shape.

FIGURE B-20

e. Duplicate the grouped triangle shape object, then rotate the new object to the left 90°.

f. Duplicate the rotated grouped triangle shape object, then move the two new triangle shape objects on the slide as shown in **FIGURE B-20**.

g. Set the guides back to 0.00, remove the guides from your screen, remove the rulers, then save your work.

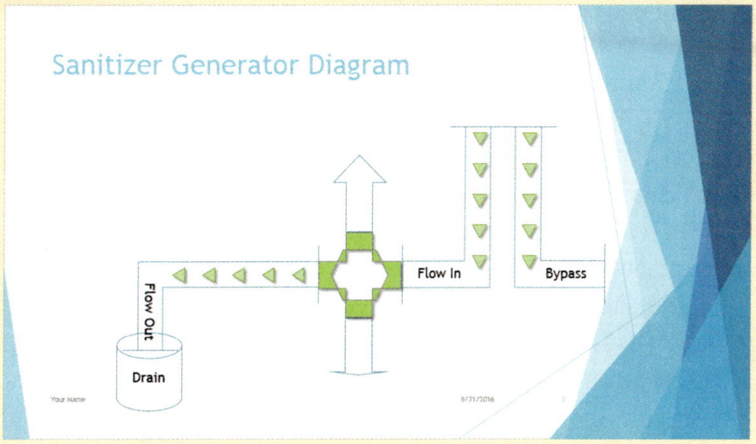

8. **Add slide footers.**

a. Open the Header and Footer dialog box.

b. On the Slide tab, click the Date and time check box to select it, then click the Fixed option button.

c. Add the slide number to the footer.

d. Type your name in the Footer text box.

e. Apply the footer to all of the slides except the title slide.

f. Open the Header and Footer dialog box again, then click the Notes and Handouts tab.

g. Click the Date and time check box, then type today's date in the Fixed text box.

h. Type the name of your class in the Header text box, then click the Page number check box.

i. Type your name in the Footer text box.

j. Apply the header and footer information to all the notes and handouts, then save your changes.

k. Submit your presentation to your instructor, close the presentation, then exit PowerPoint.

Independent Challenge 1

You are the director of the Performing Arts Center in Baton Rouge, Louisiana, and one of your many duties is to raise funds to cover operation costs. One of the primary ways you do this is by speaking to businesses, community clubs, and other organizations throughout the region. Every year you speak to many organizations, where you give a short presentation detailing what the theater center plans to do for the coming season. You need to continue working on the presentation you started already.

a. Start PowerPoint, open the presentation PPT B-3.pptx from the location where you store your Data Files, and save it as **PPT B-Center**.

b. Use Outline view to enter the following as bulleted text on the Commitment to Excellence slide:
   Excellence
   Testing
   Study
   Diligence

c. Apply the Ion Boardroom design theme to the presentation.

d. Change the font color of each play name on Slide 3 to Orange, Accent 4.

e. Change the bulleted text on Slide 5 to the Vertical Box List SmartArt Graphic, then apply the Inset SmartArt style.

f. Add your name and slide number as a footer on the slides, then save your changes.

g. Submit your presentation to your instructor, close your presentation, then exit PowerPoint.

Independent Challenge 2

You are a manager for RC Investments Inc., a financial services company. You have been asked by your boss to develop a presentation outlining important details and aspects of the mortgage process to be used at a financial seminar.

a. Start PowerPoint, open the presentation PPT B-4.pptx from the location where you store your Data Files, and save it as **PPT B-RC Investments**.

b. Apply an Office Theme Dark design theme to the presentation.

c. On Slide 4 select the three shapes, Banks, Mortgage Bankers, and Private Investors, release [Shift], then using the Align command distribute them vertically and align them to their left edges.

d. Select the blank shape, type **Borrower**, press [Shift], select the Mortgage Broker and Mortgage Bankers shapes, release [Shift], then using the Align command distribute them horizontally and align them to the middle.

e. Select all of the shapes, then apply Moderate Effect – Orange, Accent 2 from the Shape Styles group.

f. Create a diamond shape, then merge it with the Borrower shape as shown in **FIGURE B-21**.

g. Using the Arrow shape from the Shapes gallery, draw a 4 1/2-pt arrow between all of the shapes. (*Hint*: Draw one arrow shape, change the line weight using the Shape Outline list arrow, then duplicate the shape.)

h. Group all the shapes together.

i. Add the page number and your name as a footer on the notes and handouts, then save your changes.

j. Submit your presentation to your instructor, close your presentation, then exit PowerPoint.

FIGURE B-21

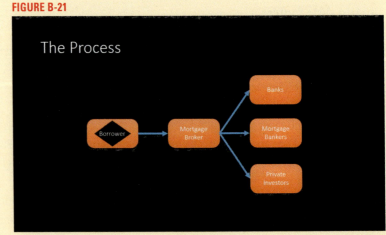

Independent Challenge 3

You are an independent distributor of natural foods in Eugene, Oregon. Your business, Coast Natural Foods, has grown progressively since its inception 10 years ago, but sales have leveled off over the last 12 months. In an effort to stimulate growth, you decide to purchase Gemco Foods Inc., a natural food dealer in Idaho and Washington, which would allow your company to begin expanding into surrounding states. Use PowerPoint to develop a presentation you can use to gain a financial backer for the acquisition. Create your own information for the presentation.

a. Start PowerPoint, create a new presentation, then apply the Wisp design theme to the presentation.
b. Type **A Plan for Growth** as the main title on the title slide, and **Coast Natural Foods** as the subtitle.
c. Save the presentation as **PPT B-Natural Foods** to the location where you store your Data Files.
d. Add five more slides with the following titles: Slide 2, **History**; Slide 3, **Trends**; Slide 4, **Growth**; Slide 5, **Funding**; Slide 6, **Management Team**.
e. Enter appropriate text into the text placeholders of the slides. Use both the Slide pane and Outline view to enter text.
f. Convert text on one slide to a SmartArt graphic, then apply the SmartArt graphic style Inset Effect.
g. Create two shapes, format the shapes, then merge the shapes together.
h. View the presentation as a slide show, then view the slides in Slide Sorter view.
i. Add the slide number and your name as a footer on the slides, then save your changes.
j. Submit your presentation to your instructor, close your presentation, then exit PowerPoint.

Independent Challenge 4: Explore

Your computer instructor at Tri-Cities College has been asked by the department head to convert her Computer Basics 101 course into an accelerated night course designed for adult students. Your instructor has asked you to help her create a presentation for the class that she can post on the Internet. Most of the basic text information is already on the slides, you primarily need to add a theme and other object formatting.

a. Start PowerPoint, open the presentation PPT B-5.pptx from the location where you store your Data Files, and save it as **PPT B-Computer 101**.
b. Add a new slide after the Course Facts slide with the same layout, type **Course Details** in the title text placeholder, then enter the following as bulleted text in Outline view:
   Information systems
   Networking
   Applied methods
   Technology solutions
   Software design
   Applications
c. Apply the Savon design theme to the presentation.
d. Select the title text object on Slide 1 (*Hint*: Press [Shift] to select the whole object), then change the text color to Orange.
e. Change the font of the title text object to FELIX TITLING, then decrease the font size to 40.
f. Click the subtitle text object on Slide 1, then change the character spacing to Loose.
g. Change the text on Slide 4 to a SmartArt graphic. Use an appropriate diagram type for a list.
h. Change the style of the SmartArt diagram using one of the SmartArt Styles, then view the presentation in Slide Show view.
i. Add the slide number and your name as a footer on the notes and handouts, then save your changes.
j. Submit your presentation to your instructor, close your presentation, then exit PowerPoint.

Visual Workshop

Create the presentation shown in **FIGURE B-22** and **FIGURE B-23**. Add today's date as the date on the title slide. Save the presentation as **PPT B-Ohio Trade** to the location where you store your Data Files. (*Hint*: The SmartArt style used for the SmartArt is a 3D style.) Review your slides in Slide Show view, then add your name as a footer to the notes and handouts. Submit your presentation to your instructor, save your changes, close the presentation, then exit PowerPoint.

FIGURE B-22

FIGURE B-23

Inserting Objects into a Presentation

CASE ▶ In this unit, you continue working on the presentation by inserting text from Microsoft Word and visual elements, including a photograph, table, and a chart, into the presentation. You format these objects using PowerPoint's powerful object-editing features.

Unit Objectives

After completing this unit, you will be able to:

- Insert text from Microsoft Word
- Insert and style a picture
- Insert a text box
- Insert a chart

- Enter and edit chart data
- Insert slides from other presentations
- Insert a table
- Insert and format WordArt

Files You Will Need

PPT C-1.pptx	PPT C-10.pptx
PPT C-2.docx	PPT C-11.pptx
PPT C-3.jpg	PPT C-12.jpg
PPT C-4.pptx	PPT C-13.pptx
PPT C-5.pptx	PPT C-14.docx
PPT C-6.docx	PPT C-15.jpg
PPT C-7.jpg	PPT C-16.jpg
PPT C-8.pptx	PPT C-17.jpg
PPT C-9.pptx	PPT C-18.jpg

Insert Text from Microsoft Word

Learning Outcomes
• Create slides using Outline view
• Move and delete slides

It is easy to insert documents saved in Microsoft Word format (.docx), Rich Text Format (.rtf), plain text format (.txt), and HTML format (.htm) into a PowerPoint presentation. If you have an outline saved in a document file, you can import it into PowerPoint to create a new presentation or create additional slides in an existing presentation. When you import a document into a presentation, PowerPoint creates an outline structure based on the styles in the document. For example, a Heading 1 style in the Word document becomes a slide title and a Heading 2 style becomes the first level of text in a bulleted list. If you insert a plain text format document into a presentation, PowerPoint creates an outline based on the tabs at the beginning of the document's paragraphs. Paragraphs without tabs become slide titles, and paragraphs with one tab indent become first-level text in bulleted lists. **CASE** ▶ *You have a Microsoft Word document with information about intercontinental Canadian train routes that you want to insert into your presentation to create several new slides.*

STEPS

1. **Start PowerPoint, open the presentation PPT C-1.pptx from the location where you store your Data Files, save it as PPT C-QST, click the VIEW tab on the Ribbon, then click the Outline View button in the Presentation Views group**

2. **Click the Slide 4 icon** ☐ **in the Outline pane, click the HOME tab on the Ribbon, click the New Slide button list arrow in the Slides group, then click Slides from Outline**

   Slide 4 appears in the Slide pane. The Insert Outline dialog box opens. Before you insert an outline into a presentation, you need to determine where you want the new slides to be placed. You want the text from the Word document inserted as new slides after Slide 4.

3. **Navigate to the location where you store your Data Files, click the Word document file PPT C-2.docx, then click Insert**

   Six new slides (5, 6, 7, 8, 9 and 10) are added to the presentation, and the new Slide 5 appears in the Slide pane. See **FIGURE C-1**.

4. **Click the down scroll arrow** ▼ **in the Outline pane and read the text for all the new slides, then click the Normal button** 🄴 **on the status bar**

   The information on Slides 5 and 6 refer to obsolete train routes and are not needed for this presentation.

5. **Press [Shift], click the Slide 6 thumbnail in the Thumbnails pane, then click the Cut button in the Clipboard group**

   Slides 5 and 6 are deleted, and the next slide down (Explorer's Trail West) becomes the new Slide 5 and appears in the Slide pane.

6. **Click the Slide 6 thumbnail in the Thumbnails pane, then drag it above Slide 5**

   Slide 6 and Slide 5 change places. All of the new slides in the presentation now follow the same theme. You want the text of the inserted outline to adopt the theme fonts of the presentation.

7. **Press [Shift], click the Slide 8 thumbnail in the Thumbnails pane, release [Shift], click the Reset button in the Slides group, then click the Save button** 🖫 **on the Quick Access toolbar**

   Notice the font type and formatting attributes of the slide text changes to reflect the current theme fonts for the presentation. The Reset button resets the slide placeholders to their default position, size, and text formatting based on the Organic presentation design theme. Compare your screen to **FIGURE C-2**.

FIGURE C-1: Outline pane showing imported text

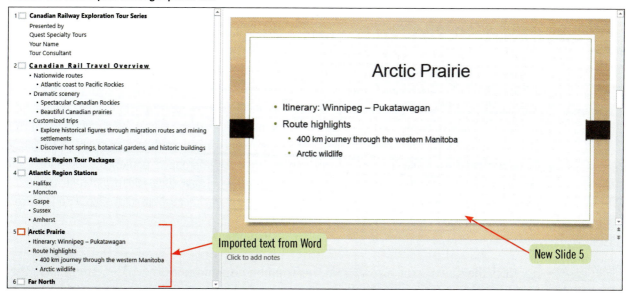

FIGURE C-2: Slides reset to Organic theme default settings

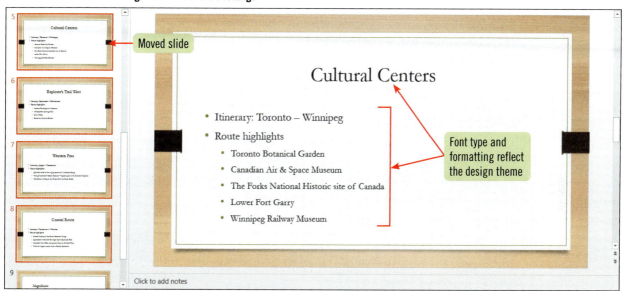

Sending a presentation using email

You can send a copy of a presentation over the Internet to a reviewer to edit and add comments. You can use Microsoft Outlook to send your presentation. Although your email program allows you to attach files, you can send a presentation using Outlook from within PowerPoint. Click the FILE tab, click Share, click Email in the center pane, then click Send as Attachment. Outlook opens and automatically creates an email with a copy of the presentation attached to it. You can also attach and send a PDF copy or an XPS copy of the presentation using your email program. Both of these file formats preserve document formatting, enable file sharing, and can be viewed online and printed.

Insert and Style a Picture

In PowerPoint, a **picture** is defined as a digital photograph, a piece of line art or clip art, or other artwork that is created in another program. PowerPoint gives you the ability to insert 14 different types of pictures including JPEG File Interchange Format and BMP Windows Bitmap files into a PowerPoint presentation. As with all objects in PowerPoint, you can format and style inserted pictures to help them fit the theme of your presentation. You can also hide a portion of the picture you don't want to be seen by **cropping** it. The cropped portion of a picture is still available to you if you ever want to show that part of picture again. To reduce the size of the file you can permanently delete the cropped portion by applying picture compression settings in the Compress Pictures dialog box. **CASE** ▶ *Using your digital camera, you took photographs during your train tours. In this lesson you insert a picture that you saved as a JPG file on your computer, and then you crop and style it to best fit the slide.*

STEPS

1. **Click the down scroll arrow ▼ in the Thumbnails pane, click the Slide 9 thumbnail, then click the Pictures icon in the content placeholder on the slide**

   The Insert Picture dialog box opens displaying the pictures available in the default Pictures library.

2. **Navigate to location where you store your Data Files, select the picture file PPT C-3.jpg, then click Insert**

   The picture fills the content placeholder on the slide, and the PICTURE TOOLS FORMAT tab opens on the Ribbon. The picture would look better if you cropped some of the image.

3. **Click the Crop button in the Size group, then place the pointer over the lower-right corner cropping handle of the picture**

   The pointer changes to ⌐. When the Crop button is active, cropping handles appear next to the sizing handles on the selected object.

4. **Drag the corner of the picture up and to the left as shown in FIGURE C-3, release the mouse button, then press [Esc]**

   PowerPoint has a number of picture formatting options, and you decide to experiment with some of them.

5. **Click the More button ▼ in the Picture Styles group, move your pointer over the style thumbnails in the gallery to see how the different styles change the picture, then click Rotated, White (3rd row)**

   The picture now has a white frame and is rotated slightly to the left.

6. **Click the Corrections button in the Adjust group, move your pointer over the thumbnails to see how the picture changes, then click Sharpen: 50% in the Sharpen/Soften section**

   The picture clarity is better.

7. **Click the Artistic Effects button in the Adjust group, move your pointer over the thumbnails to see how the picture changes, then click a blank area of the slide**

   The artistic effects are all interesting, but none of them will work well for this picture.

8. **Drag the picture to the center of the blank area of the slide, click a blank area on the slide, then save your changes**

   Compare your screen to FIGURE C-4.

Inserting Objects into a Presentation

FIGURE C-3: Using the cropping pointer to crop a picture

FIGURE C-4: Cropped and styled picture

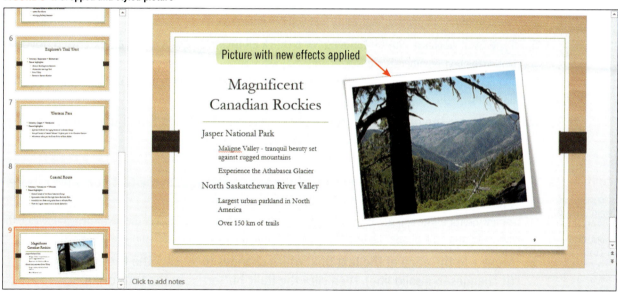

Saving slides as graphics

You can save PowerPoint slides as graphics and later use them in other presentations, in graphics programs, and on Web pages. Display the slide you want to save, click the FILE tab, then click Save As. Select the location where you want to save the file. In the Save As dialog box, click the Save as type list arrow, select the desired graphics format, then name the file. Graphics format choices include GIF Graphics Interchange Format (*.gif), JPEG File Interchange Format (*.jpg), PNG Portable Network Graphics Format (*.png), TIFF Tag Image File Format (*.tif), and Device Independent Bitmap (*.bmp). Click Save, then click the desired option when the alert box appears asking if you want to save all the slides or only the current slide.

Insert a Text Box

As you've already learned, you enter text on a slide using a title or content placeholder that is arranged on the slide based on a slide layout. Every so often you need additional text on a slide where the traditional placeholder does not place text effectively for your message. You can create an individual text box by clicking the Text Box button in the Text group on the INSERT tab on the Ribbon. There are two types of text boxes that you can create: a text label, used for a small phrase where text doesn't automatically wrap to the next line inside the box, and a word-processing box, used for a sentence or paragraph where the text wraps inside the boundaries of the box. Either type of text box can be formatted and edited just like any other text object. **CASE** ▶ *You decide to add a text box to the SmartArt graphic on Slide 3. You create a word-processing box on the slide, enter text, edit text, and then format the text.*

STEPS

1. Click the **Slide 3 thumbnail** in the Thumbnails pane, click the **INSERT tab** on the Ribbon, then click the **Text Box button** in the Text group
   The pointer changes to ↓.

2. Move ↓ to the blank area of the slide to the left of the SmartArt graphic, then drag the pointer ┼ down and toward the right about 3" to create a text box
   When you begin dragging, an outline of the text box appears, indicating the size of the text box you are drawing. After you release the mouse button, a blinking insertion point appears inside the text box, in this case a word-processing box, indicating that you can enter text.

3. Type **Each package can be tailored for a quick all-inclusive getaway or an extended holiday**
   Notice the text box increases in size as your text wraps to additional lines inside the text box. Your screen should look similar to **FIGURE C-5**. After entering the text, you realize the sentence could be clearer if written differently.

4. Drag I over the phrase **all-inclusive** to select it, position ⬉ on top of the selected phrase, then press and hold the **left mouse button**
   The pointer changes to ⬉.

5. Drag the selected words to the left of the word "package" in the text box, then release the mouse button
   A grey insertion line appears as you drag, indicating where PowerPoint places the text when you release the mouse button. The phrase "all-inclusive" moves before the word "package" and is still selected.

6. Move I to the edge of the text box, which changes to ⬉, click the **text box border** (it changes to a solid line), then click the **Italic button** *I* in the Font group
   All of the text in the text box is italicized.

7. Click the **Shape Fill list arrow** in the Drawing group, click the **Blue-Gray, Accent 3, Lighter 60% color box**, click the **Shape Outline list arrow** in the Drawing group, then click the **Orange, Accent 5 color box**
   The text object is now filled with a light blue color and has a light orange outline.

8. Drag the **right-middle sizing handle** of the text box to the right until all the text fits on two lines, position ⬉ over the text box edge, then drag the **text box** to the Smart Guide on the slide as shown in **FIGURE C-6**

9. Click the **Reading View button** 📖 on the status bar, review the slide, press **[Esc]**, then save your changes

FIGURE C-5: New text object

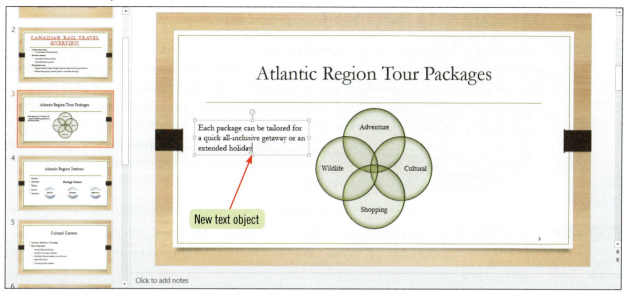

FIGURE C-6: Formatted text object

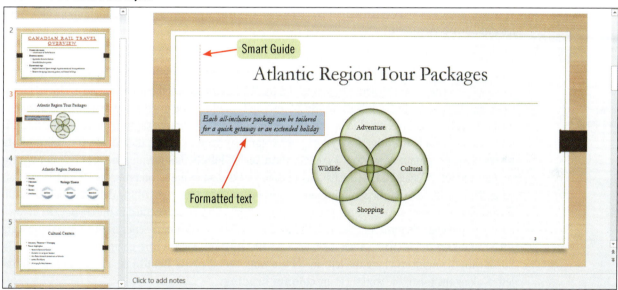

Changing text box defaults

You can change the default formatting characteristics of text boxes you create using the Text Box button on the INSERT tab. To change the formatting defaults for text boxes, select an existing formatted text box, or create a new one and format it using any of PowerPoint's formatting commands. When you are ready to change the text box defaults, press [Shift], right-click the formatted text box, release [Shift], then click Set as Default Text Box on the shortcut menu. Any new text boxes you create now will display the formatting characteristics of this formatted text box.

Insert a Chart

Frequently, the best way to communicate numerical information is with a visual aid such as a chart. PowerPoint uses Excel to create charts. A **chart** is the graphical representation of numerical data. Every chart has a corresponding **worksheet** that contains the numerical data displayed by the chart. When you insert a chart object into PowerPoint, you are actually embedding it. An **embedded object** is one that is a part of your presentation (just like any other object you insert into PowerPoint) except that an embedded object's data source can be opened, in this case using Excel, for editing purposes. Changes you make to an embedded object in PowerPoint using the features in PowerPoint do not affect the data source for the data. **CASE** ▶ *You insert a chart on a new slide.*

STEPS

1. **Click the Slide 9 thumbnail in the Thumbnails pane, then press [Enter]**

   Pressing [Enter] adds a new slide to your presentation with the slide layout of the selected slide, in this case the Content with Caption slide layout.

2. **Click the HOME tab on the Ribbon, click the Layout button in the Slides group, then click Title and Content**

   The slide layout changes to the Title and Content layout.

3. **Click the Title placeholder, type Customer Survey, then click the Insert Chart icon ⬛ in the Content placeholder**

   The Insert Chart dialog box opens as shown in **FIGURE C-7**. Each chart type includes a number of 2D and 3D styles. The Clustered Column chart is the default 2D chart style. For a brief explanation of chart types, refer to **TABLE C-1**.

4. **Click OK**

   The PowerPoint window displays a clustered column chart below a worksheet with sample data, as shown in **FIGURE C-8**. The CHART TOOLS DESIGN tab on the Ribbon contains commands you use in PowerPoint to work with the chart. The worksheet consists of rows and columns. The intersection of a row and a column is called a **cell**. Cells are referred to by their row and column location; for example, the cell at the intersection of column A and row 1 is called cell A1. Each column and row of data in the worksheet is called a **data series**. Cells in column A and row 1 contain **data series labels** that identify the data or values in the column and row. "Category 1" is the data series label for the data in the second row, and "Series 1" is a data series label for the data in the second column. Cells below and to the right of the data series labels, in the shaded blue portion of the worksheet, contain the data values that are represented in the chart. Cells in row 1 appear in the chart **legend** and describe the data in the series. Each data series has corresponding **data series markers** in the chart, which are graphical representations such as bars, columns, or pie wedges. The boxes with the numbers along the left side of the worksheet are **row headings**, and the boxes with the letters along the top of the worksheet are **column headings**.

5. **Move the pointer over the worksheet, then click cell C4**

   The pointer changes to ✛. Cell C4, containing the value 1.8, is the selected cell, which means it is now the **active cell**. The active cell has a thick green border around it.

6. **Click the Close button ✖ on the worksheet title bar, then click the Quick Layout button in the Chart Layouts group**

   The worksheet window closes, and the Quick Layout gallery opens.

7. **Move ▷ over all the layouts in the gallery, then click Layout 1**

   This new layout moves the legend to the right side of the chart and increases the size of the data series markers.

8. **Click in a blank area of the slide to deselect the chart, then save your changes**

   The CHART TOOLS DESIGN tab is no longer active.

Inserting Objects into a Presentation

FIGURE C-7: Insert Chart dialog box

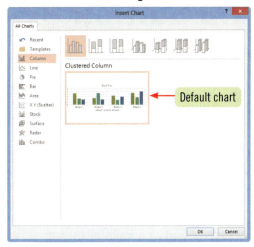

FIGURE C-8: Worksheet open with data for the chart

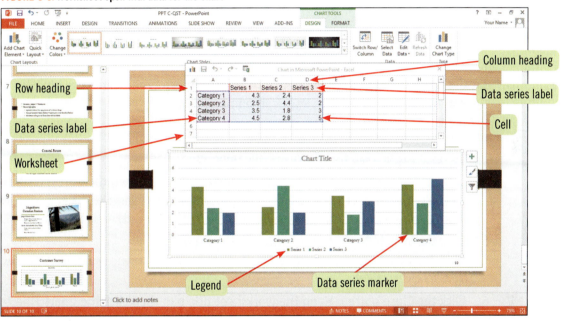

TABLE C-1: Chart types

chart type	icon looks like	use to
Column		Track values over time or across categories
Line		Track values over time
Pie		Compare individual values to the whole
Bar		Compare values in categories or over time
Area		Show contribution of each data series to the total over time
X Y (Scatter)		Compare pairs of values
Stock		Show stock market information or scientific data
Surface		Show value trends across two dimensions
Radar		Show changes in values in relation to a center point
Combo		Use multiple types of data markers to compare values

Inserting Objects into a Presentation

Enter and Edit Chart Data

Learning Outcomes
• Change chart data values
• Format a chart

After you insert a chart into your presentation, you need to replace the sample information with the correct data. If you have data in an Excel worksheet, you can import it from Excel; otherwise, you can type your own data into the worksheet. As you enter data and make other changes in the worksheet, the chart on the slide automatically reflects the new changes. **CASE** *You enter and format survey data you collected that asked people to positively rate four train tours with respect to three factors: suite accommodations, food quality, and overall trip satisfaction.*

STEPS

1. **Click the chart on Slide 10, then click the Edit Data button in the Data group on the CHART TOOLS DESIGN tab on the Ribbon**
   The chart is selected and the worksheet opens in a separate window. The information in the worksheet needs to be replaced with the correct data.

2. **Click the Series 1 cell, type Suite, press [Tab], type Food, press [Tab], then type Overall**
   The data series labels, describing three survey factors, are entered in the worksheet and display in the legend on the chart. Pressing [Tab] moves the active cell from left to right one cell at a time in a row. Pressing [Enter] in the worksheet moves the active cell down one cell at a time in a column.

3. **Click the Category 1 cell, type Atlantic, press [Enter], type Prairie, press [Enter], type Rockies, press [Enter], type Pacific, then press [Enter]**
   The data series labels, describing the tour regions, are entered in the worksheet and appear along the bottom of the chart on the x-axis. The x-axis is the horizontal axis also referred to as the **category axis**, and the y-axis is the vertical axis also referred to as the **value axis**.

4. **Enter the data shown in FIGURE C-9 to complete the worksheet, then press [Enter]**
   Notice that the height of each column in the chart, as well as the values along the y-axis, adjust to reflect the numbers you typed. You have finished entering the data in the Excel worksheet.

5. **Click the Switch Row/Column button in the Data group**
   The data charted on the x-axis switches with the y-axis. Notice the legend now displays the row data series labels for each tour region.

6. **Click the Close button on the worksheet title bar, then click the Chart Title text box object in the chart**
   The worksheet window closes.

7. **Type Guest Satisfaction, click a blank area of the chart, then click the Chart Styles button to the right of the chart to open the Chart Styles gallery**
   The Chart Styles gallery opens on the left side of the chart with STYLE selected.

8. **Scroll down the gallery, click Style 6, click COLOR at the top of the Chart Styles gallery, then click Color 2 in the Colorful section**
   The new chart style and color gives the column data markers a professional look as shown in FIGURE C-10.

9. **Click a blank area on the slide, then save the presentation**
   The Chart Styles gallery closes.

FIGURE C-9: Worksheet data for the chart

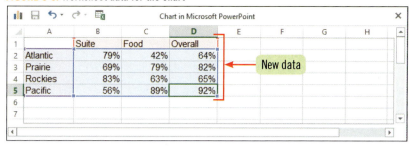

FIGURE C-10: Formatted chart

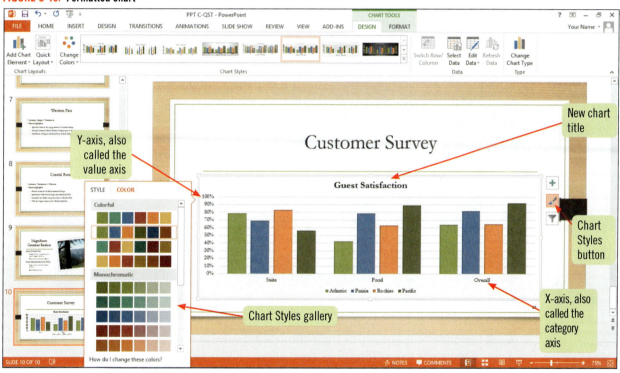

Adding a hyperlink to a chart

You can add a hyperlink to any object in PowerPoint, including a chart. Select that chart, click the INSERT tab on the Ribbon, then click the Hyperlink button in the Links group. If you are linking to another file, click the Existing File or Web Page button, locate the file you want to link to the chart, then click OK. Or, if you want to link to another slide in the presentation, click the Place in This Document button, click the slide in the list, then click OK. Now, during a slide show you can click the chart to open the linked object. To remove the link, click the chart, click the Hyperlink button in the Links group, then click Remove Link.

Insert Slides from Other Presentations

To save time and energy, you can insert one or more slides you already created in other presentations into an existing presentation or one you are currently working on. One way to share slides between presentations is to open an existing presentation, copy the slides you want to the Clipboard, and then paste them into your open presentation. However, PowerPoint offers a simpler way to transfer slides directly between presentations. By using the Reuse Slides pane, you can insert slides from another presentation or a network location called a Slide Library. A **Slide Library** is folder that you and others can access to open, modify, and review presentation slides. Newly inserted slides automatically take on the theme of the open presentation, unless you decide to use slide formatting from the original source presentation. **CASE** ▶ *You decide to insert slides you created for another presentation into the Canadian train tour presentation.*

STEPS

1. **Click the Slide 4 thumbnail in the Thumbnails pane, click the New Slide list arrow in the Slides group, then click Reuse Slides**

   The Reuse Slides pane opens on the right side of the presentation window.

2. **Click the Browse button in the Reuse Slides pane, click Browse File, navigate to the location where you store your Data Files, select the presentation file PPT C-4.pptx, then click Open**

   Six slide thumbnails are displayed in the pane with the first slide thumbnail selected as shown in **FIGURE C-11**. The slide thumbnails identify the slides in the **source presentation**, PPT C-4.pptx.

3. **Point to each slide in the Reuse Slides pane list to display a preview of the slide, then click the Manitoba Tour slide**

   The new slide appears in the Thumbnails pane and Slide pane in your current presentation as the new Slide 5. Notice the new slide assumes the design style and formatting of your presentation, which is called the **destination presentation**.

4. **Click the Keep source formatting check box at the bottom of the Reuse Slides pane, click the Northern Quebec Tour slide, then click the Keep source formatting check box**

   This new slide keeps the design style and formatting of the source presentation.

5. **Click the Slide 4 thumbnail in the Thumbnails pane, in the Reuse Slides pane click the Trans Canadian Luxury Tour slide, then click the Southern Ontario Tour slide**

   Two more slides are inserted into the presentation with the design style and formatting of the destination presentation. You realize that slides 6 and 8 are not needed for this presentation.

6. **With the Slide 6 thumbnail still selected in the Thumbnails pane, press [Ctrl], click the Slide 8 thumbnail, release [Ctrl], right-click the Slide 8 thumbnail, then click Delete Slide in the shortcut menu**

   Slides 6 and 8 are deleted. Objects on the inserted slides may not be in the correct position on the slide. To ensure objects are positioned correctly on the slide, you can reset the slide defaults.

7. **Click the Slide 6 thumbnail in the Thumbnails pane, press [Shift], click the Slide 5 thumbnail, release [Shift], then click the Reset button in the Slides group**

   The selected slides are set back to the original default settings for this design theme.

8. **Click the Reuse Slides pane Close button ☒, then save the presentation**

   The Reuse Slides pane closes. Compare your screen to **FIGURE C-12**.

FIGURE C-11: Presentation window with Reuse Slides pane open

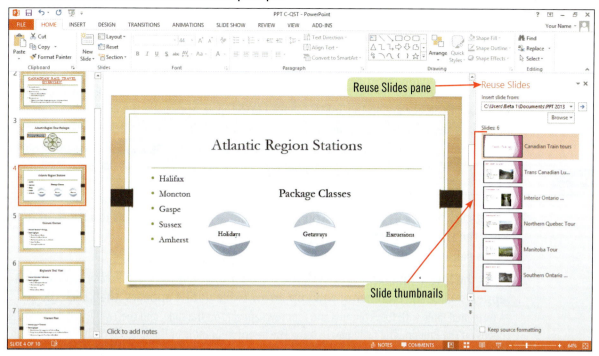

FIGURE C-12: New slides with correct design

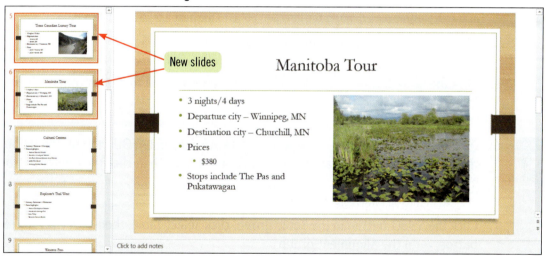

Working with multiple windows

Another way to work with information in multiple presentations is to arrange the presentation windows on your monitor so you see each window side by side. Open each presentation, click the VIEW tab on the Ribbon in any presentation window, then click the Arrange All button in the Window group. Each presentation you have open is placed next to each other so you can easily drag, or transfer, information between the presentations. If you are working with more than two open presentations, you can overlap the presentation windows on top of one another. Open all the presentations you want, then click the Cascade Windows button in the Window group. Now you can to easily jump from one presentation to another by clicking on the presentation title bar or any part of the presentation window.

Insert a Table

Learning Outcomes
• Insert a table
• Add text to a table
• Change table size and layout

As you create your presentation, you may have some information that would look best organized in rows and columns. For example, if you want to compare the basic details of different train accommodations side by side, a table is ideal for this type of information. Once you have created a table, two new tabs, the TABLE TOOLS DESIGN tab and the TABLE TOOLS LAYOUT tab, appear on the Ribbon. You can use the commands on the table tabs to apply color styles, change cell borders, add cell effects, add rows and columns to your table, adjust the size of cells, and align text in the cells. **CASE** *You decide a table best illustrates the different levels of accommodation services offered by the train tour company.*

STEPS

1. **Right-click** Slide 4 **in the Slides Thumbnails pane, click** New Slide **on the shortcut menu, click the** title placeholder**, then type** Accommodations

   A new slide with the Title and Content layout appears.

2. **Click the** Insert Table icon **, click the** Number of columns down arrow **once until** 4 **appears, click the** Number of rows up arrow **twice until** 4 **appears, then click** OK

   A formatted table with four columns and four rows appears on the slide, and the TABLE TOOLS DESIGN tab opens on the Ribbon. The table has 16 cells. The insertion point is in the first cell of the table and is ready to accept text.

   > **QUICK TIP**
   > Press [Tab] when the insertion point is in the last cell of a table to create a new row.

3. **Type** Classic**, press [Tab], type** Deluxe**, press [Tab], type** Luxury**, press [Tab], type** Business**, then press [Tab]**

   The text you typed appears in the top four cells of the table. Pressing [Tab] moves the insertion point to the next cell; pressing [Enter] moves the insertion point to the next line in the same cell.

4. **Enter the rest of the table information shown in** FIGURE C-13

   The table would look better if it were formatted differently.

5. **Click the** More button **in the Table Styles group, scroll to the bottom of the gallery, then click** Dark Style 1 – Accent 3

   The background and text color change to reflect the table style you applied.

   > **QUICK TIP**
   > Change the height or width of any table cell by dragging its borders.

6. **Click the** Classic cell **in the table, click the** TABLE TOOLS LAYOUT tab **on the Ribbon, click the** Select button **in the Table group, click** Select Row**, then click the** Center button **in the Alignment group**

   The text in the top row is centered horizontally in each cell.

7. **Click the** Select button **in the Table group, click** Select Table**, then click the** Align Bottom button **in the Alignment group**

   The text in the entire table is aligned at the bottom within each cell.

   > **QUICK TIP**
   > To change the cell color behind text, click the Shading list arrow in the Table Styles group, then choose a color.

8. **Click the** TABLE TOOLS DESIGN tab**, click the** Effects button **in the Table Styles group, point to** Cell Bevel**, then click** Convex **(2nd row)**

   The 3D effect makes the cells of the table stand out. The table would look better in a different place on the slide.

9. **Place the pointer over the top edge of the table, drag the table straight down as shown in** FIGURE C-14**, click a blank area of the slide, then save the presentation**

   The slide looks better with more space between the table and the slide title.

FIGURE C-13: Inserted table with data

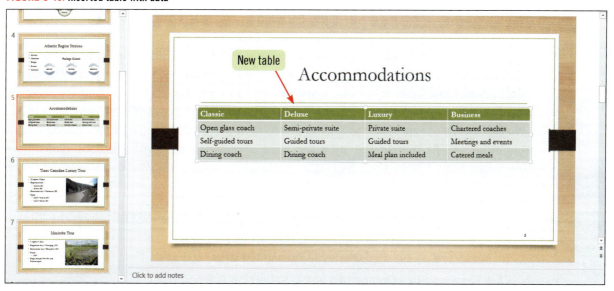

FIGURE C-14: Formatted table

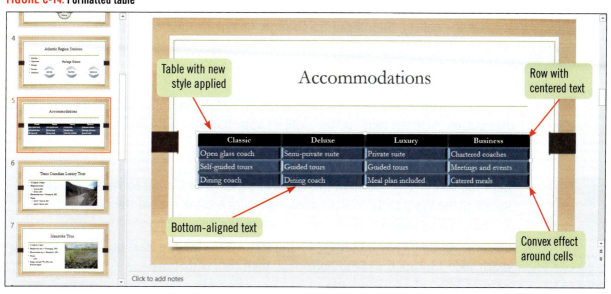

Drawing tables

Choose the slide where you want the table, click the Table button in the Tables group on the Insert tab, then click Draw Table. The pointer changes to ✐. Drag to define the boundaries of the table in the area of the slide where you want the table. A dotted outline appears as you draw . Next, you draw to create the rows and columns of your table. Click the TABLE TOOLS DESIGN tab on the Ribbon, click the Draw Table button in the Draw Borders group, then draw lines for columns and rows. Be sure to draw within the boundary line of the table. You can also create a table by clicking the Table button in the Tables group on the Insert tab, then dragging ⌖ over the table grid to create a table.

Insert and Format WordArt

As you work to create an interesting presentation, your goal should include making your slides visually appealing. Sometimes plain text can come across as dull and unexciting in a presentation. **WordArt** is a set of decorative text styles, or text effects, you can apply to any text object to help direct the attention of your audience to a certain piece of information. You can use WordArt in two different ways: you can apply a WordArt text style to an existing text object that converts the text into WordArt, or you can create a new WordArt object. The WordArt text styles and effects include text shadows, reflections, glows, bevels, 3D rotations, and transformations. **CASE** ▸ *Use WordArt to create a new WordArt text object on Slide 8.*

STEPS

1. **Click the Slide 8 thumbnail in the Thumbnails pane, click the INSERT tab on the Ribbon, then click the WordArt button in the Text group**
   The WordArt gallery appears displaying 20 WordArt text styles.

2. **Click Gradient Fill – Orange, Accent 1, Reflection (second row)**
   A text object appears in the middle of the slide displaying sample text with the WordArt style you just selected. Notice the DRAWING TOOLS FORMAT tab is open on the Ribbon.

3. **Click the edge of the WordArt text object, then when the pointer changes to ⁺↖, drag the text object to the blank area of the slide**

4. **Click the More button ▼ in the WordArt Styles group, move ↳ over all of the WordArt styles in the gallery, then click Fill – Orange, Accent 1, Outline – Background 1, Hard Shadow – Accent 1**
   The WordArt Styles change the sample text in the WordArt text object. The new WordArt style is applied to the text object.

5. **Drag to select the text Your text here in the WordArt text object, click the Decrease Font Size button A˅ in the Mini toolbar until 44 appears in the Font Size text box, type Best Value, press [Enter], then type Of the Summer**
   The text is smaller and appears on two lines.

6. **Click the Text Effects button in the WordArt Styles group, point to Transform, click Inflate in the Warp section (sixth row), then click a blank area of the slide**
   The inflate effect is applied to the text object. Compare your screen to **FIGURE C-15**.

7. **Click the Reading View button 📖 on the status bar, click the Next button ⏵ until you reach Slide 13, click the Menu button 📑, then click End Show**

8. **Click the Slide Sorter button ▦ on the status bar, then click the Zoom Out icon ➖ on the status bar until all 13 slides are visible**
   Compare your screen with **FIGURE C-16**.

9. **Click the Normal button 🔲 on the status bar, add your name and the date as a footer to the slides, save your changes, submit your presentation to your instructor, then exit PowerPoint**

FIGURE C-15: WordArt inserted on slide

FIGURE C-16: Completed presentation in Slide Sorter view

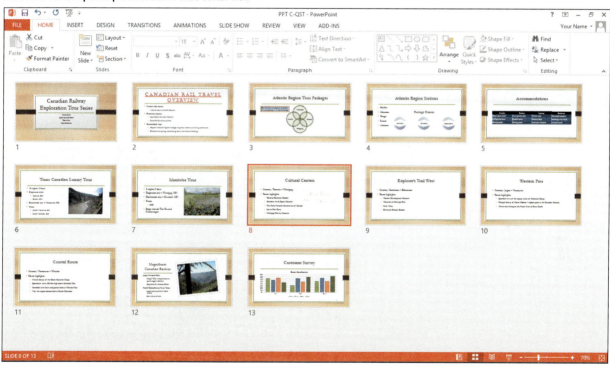

Saving a presentation as a video

You can save your PowerPoint presentation as a full-fidelity video, which incorporates all slide timings, transitions, animations, and narrations. The video can be distributed using a disc, the Web, or email. Depending on how you want to display your video, you have three resolution settings from which to choose: Computer & HD Displays, Internet & DVD, and Portable Devices. The Large setting, Computer & HD Displays (1280 X 720), is used for viewing on a computer monitor,

projector, or other high-definition displays. The Medium setting, Internet & DVD (852 X 480), is used for uploading to the Web or copying to a standard DVD. The Small setting, Portable Devices (424 X 240), is used on portable devices including portable media players such as Microsoft Zune. To save your presentation as a video, click the FILE tab, click Export, click Create a Video, choose your settings, then click the Create Video button.

Practice

Concepts Review

Label each element of the PowerPoint window shown in FIGURE C-17.

FIGURE C-17

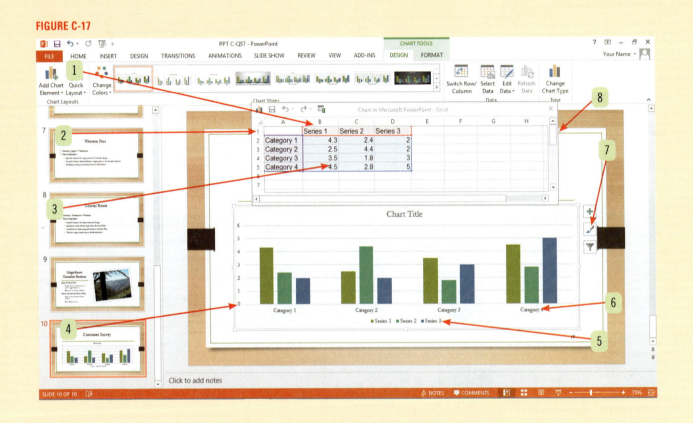

Match each term with the statement that best describes it.

9. **Picture**
10. **Worksheet**
11. **Data series marker**
12. **Table**
13. **Data series**

a. Each column or row of data in a worksheet

b. A digital photo or clip art

c. The graphical representation of numerical data in chart

d. Contains the numerical data displayed in a chart

e. PowerPoint object that organizes data in columns and rows

Select the best answer from the list of choices.

14. When you _____ a document into a presentation, PowerPoint creates slides from the outline based on the styles in the document.
    a. link
    b. create
    c. import
    d. package

15. According to this unit, a picture is:
    a. Created in another program.
    b. Defined as an embedded painting.
    c. Created using the Picture Tools Format tab.
    d. Only used to enhance a slide in Slide Show view.

16. A text label is best used for:
    a. WordArt.
    b. A long paragraph.
    c. A content placeholder.
    d. A small text phrase.

17. When you insert slides using the Reuse Slides pane, the current open presentation is also called the _____ presentation.
    a. reused
    b. source
    c. destination
    d. first

18. An object that has its own data source and becomes a part of your presentation after you insert it best describes which of the following?
    a. A Word outline
    b. An embedded object
    c. A WordArt object
    d. A table

19. Use _____ to apply a set of decorative text styles or text effects to text.
    a. a picture
    b. rich text format
    c. a hyperlink
    d. WordArt

20. A simple way to insert slides from another presentation is to use the _____ pane.
    a. Insert Slides
    b. Reuse Slides
    c. Slides Group
    d. Browse

Skills Review

1. **Insert text from Microsoft Word.**
   a. Open the file PPT C-5.pptx from the location where you store your Data Files, then save it as **PPT C-Colcom**. You will work to create the completed presentation as shown in FIGURE C-18.
   b. Click Slide 3 in the Thumbnails pane, then use the Slides from Outline command to insert the file PPT C-6.docx from the location where you store your Data Files.
   c. In the Thumbnails pane, drag Slide 6 above Slide 5 then delete Slide 7, "Expansion Potential".
   d. Select Slides 4, 5, and 6 in the Slides tab, reset the slides to the default theme settings, then save your work.

FIGURE C-18

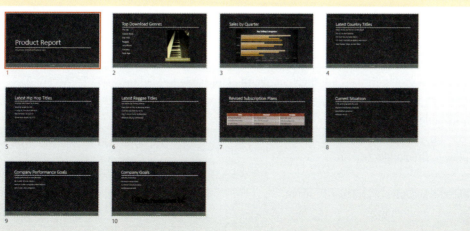

PowerPoint 2013

Skills Review (continued)

2. Insert and style a picture.

   a. Select Slide 2 in the Thumbnails pane, then insert the picture PPT C-7.jpg from the location where you store your Data Files.

   b. Crop the top portion of the picture down to the piano keys, then crop the left side of the picture about 1/4 inch.

   c. Drag the picture up so it is in the center of the blank area of the slide.

   d. Click the Color button, then change the picture color to Tan, Accent color 3 Dark.

   e. Save your changes.

3. Insert a text box.

   a. On Slide 2, insert a text box below the picture.

   b. Type **Public submissions for music up 9%**.

   c. Delete the word **for**, then drag the word **music** after the word **Public**.

   d. Select the text object, then click the More button in the Shape Styles group on the DRAWING TOOLS FORMAT tab.

   e. Click Moderate Effect – Tan, Accent 3, then fit the text box to the text by dragging its sizing handles.

   f. Center the text object under the picture using Smart Guides.

4. Insert a chart.

   a. Go to Slide 3, Sales by Quarter, click the Chart button in the Illustrations group on the INSERT tab, click Bar in the left column, then insert a Clustered Bar chart.

   b. Close the worksheet, drag the top-middle sizing handle of the chart down under the slide title, then apply the Layout 1 quick layout to the chart.

5. Enter and edit chart data.

   a. Show the worksheet, then enter the data shown in **TABLE C-2** into the worksheet.

   b. Click the Switch Row/Column button in the Data group, then close the worksheet window.

   c. Type **Top Selling Categories** in the chart title text object.

   d. Click the Chart Styles button next to the chart then change the chart style to Style 7.

   e. Click COLOR in the Charts Styles gallery, then change the color to Color 9 in the Monochromatic section.

   f. Close the Charts Styles gallery, then save your changes.

TABLE C-2

	Hip hop	Reggae	Country
1st Qtr	290,957	208,902	530,457
2nd Qtr	229,840	425,854	490,823
3rd Qtr	485,063	535,927	356,978
4th Qtr	565,113	303,750	637,902

6. Insert slides from other presentations.

   a. Make sure Slide 3 is selected, then open the Reuse Slides pane.

   b. Open the file PPT C-8.pptx from the location where you store your Data Files.

   c. Insert the second slide thumbnail, then insert the first slide thumbnail and the third thumbnail.

   d. Close the Reuse Slides pane, then using [Shift] select Slide 4 in the Thumbnails pane.

   e. Click the Reset button in the Slides group, then save your work.

7. Insert a table.

   a. Add a new slide after Slide 6 with the Title and Content layout.

   b. Add the slide title **Revised Subscription Plans**.

   c. Insert a table with three columns and four rows.

   d. Enter the information shown in **TABLE C-3**, then change the table style to Medium Style 2 – Accent 2.

   e. In the TABLE TOOLS LAYOUT tab, center the text in the top row.

   f. Select the whole table, open the TABLE TOOLS DESIGN tab, click the Effects button, point to Cell Bevel, then apply the Art Deco effect.

   g. Move the table to the center of the blank area of the slide, then save your changes.

TABLE C-3

Basic	Standard	Premium
$.99 per download	$11.99 per month	$34.99 per year
Unlimited downloads	Max. 100 downloads	Unlimited downloads
Limited access	Limited access	Unlimited access

Skills Review (continued)

8. Insert and format WordArt.

   a. Go to Slide 10, then, insert a WordArt text object using the style Fill – White, Text 1, Outline – Background 1, Hard Shadow – Background 1.

   b. Type **ColCom Productions Inc.**, then apply the WordArt style Fill – Gold, Accent 1, Outline – Background 1, Hard Shadow – Accent 1.

   c. Apply the Deflate Top Transform effect (seventh row) to the text object, then move the text object to the middle of the blank area of the slide.

   d. View the presentation in Slide Show view, add your name as a footer to all the slides, then save your changes.

   e. Submit your presentation to your instructor, close your presentation, and exit PowerPoint.

Independent Challenge 1

You are a financial management consultant for Chapman & Rowley Investments LLP, located in Nyack, New York. One of your responsibilities is to create standardized presentations on different financial investments for use on the company Web site. As part of the presentation for this meeting, you insert a chart, add a WordArt object, and insert slides from another presentation.

   a. Open the file PPT C-9.pptx from the location where you store your Data Files, then save it as **PPT C-C&R**.

   b. Add your name as the footer on all of the slides, then apply the Ion Design Theme.

   c. Insert a clustered column chart on Slide 2, then enter the data in **TABLE C-4** into the worksheet.

   d. Close the worksheet, format the chart using Style 11, then move the chart below the slide title text object.

   e. Type **Annualized Return** in the chart title text object.

   f. Open the Reuse Slides pane, open the file PPT C-10.pptx from the location where you store your Data Files, then insert slides 2, 3, and 4.

   g. Close the Reuse Slides pane, move Slide 5 above Slide 4, then select Slide 3.

   h. Insert a WordArt object with the Fill – Dark Red, Accent 1, Shadow style, type **Never too early**, press [Enter], type **To**, press [Enter], then type **Start saving**.

   i. Click the Text Effects button, point to Transform, then apply the Button text effect from the Follow Path section.

   j. Move the WordArt object to a blank area of the slide, click the Text Effects button, point to Shadow, then apply the shadow Offset Top.

   k. View the presentation slide show, make any necessary changes, then save your work. See **FIGURE C-19**.

   l. Submit the presentation to your instructor, then close the presentation, and exit PowerPoint.

TABLE C-4

	Stocks	Bonds	Mutual funds
1 Year	1.9%	1.2%	2.8%
3 Year	4.3%	3.4%	4.7%
5 Year	3.9%	2.8%	7.3%
7 Year	2.6%	3.0%	6.2%

FIGURE C-19

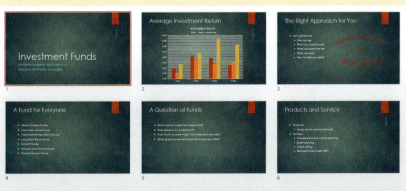

PowerPoint 2013

Independent Challenge 2

You work for Prince Rupert Harbor Group, a company in Prince Rupert, British Columbia, that oversees all of the commercial business at the Prince Rupert port. You have been asked to enhance a marketing presentation that is going to promote the port facilities. You work on completing a presentation by inserting two pictures, a text box, and a table.

a. Start PowerPoint, open the file PPT C-11.pptx from the location where you store your Data Files, and save it as **PPT C-PRHG**.

b. Add your name and today's date to Slide 1 in the Subtitle text box.

c. Apply the Wisp theme to the presentation.

d. On Slide 5, click the Pictures icon in the content placeholder, then insert the file PPT C-12.jpg from the location where you store your Data Files.

e. Apply the Double Frame, Black picture style to the picture, click the Color button, then change the color to Temperature: 8800 K (Color Tone section).

f. Insert a text box on the slide below the picture, type **2nd largest fishing fleet in Canada**, then format the text and text box with three formatting commands.

g. Go to Slide 2, select the picture, click the Picture Effects button, point to Soft Edges, then click 10 Point.

h. Open the Artistic Effects gallery, then apply the Blur effect to the picture.

i. Go to Slide 4, create a new table, then enter the data in **TABLE C-5**. Format the table using at least two formatting commands. Be able to identify which formatting commands you applied to the table.

j. View the final presentation in slide show view. Make any necessary changes (refer to **FIGURE C-20**).

k. Save the presentation, submit the presentation to your instructor, close the file, and exit PowerPoint.

TABLE C-5

Total	Aug 2016	Aug 2015	Variance
Total containers	47,524.0	43,418.0	9.5%
Loaded containers	35,283.0	34,016.5	3.7%
Empty containers	12,241.0	9,401.5	30.2%
Total tons	475,240.0	434,180.0	9.5%

FIGURE C-20

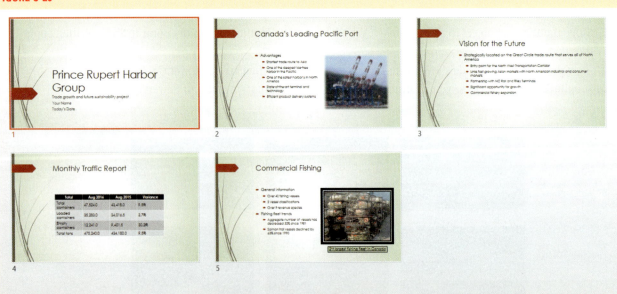

Independent Challenge 3

You work for OneGlobal Inc., a company that produces instructional software to help people learn foreign languages. Once a year, OneGlobal holds a meeting with their biggest client, the United States Department of State, to brief the government on new products and to receive feedback on existing products. Your supervisor has started a presentation and has asked you to look it over and add other elements to make it look better.

a. Start PowerPoint, open the file PPT C-13.pptx from the location where you store your Data Files, and save it as **PPT C-OneGlobal**.

b. Add an appropriate design theme to the presentation.

c. Insert the Word outline PPT C-14.docx after the Product Revisions slide.

d. Insert and format a text object and a WordArt object.

e. Insert an appropriate table on a slide of your choice. Use your own information, or use text from a bulleted list on one of the slides.

f. Insert and format at least two appropriate shapes that emphasize slide content. If appropriate, use the Align, Distribute, and Group commands to organize your shapes.

g. Add your name as footer text on the slides and the notes and handouts, then save the presentation.

h. Submit your presentation to your instructor, close the file, then exit PowerPoint.

Independent Challenge 4: Explore

You are in the Foreign Exchange Club at your college, and one of your assignments is to present information on past foreign student exchanges to different businesses and other organizations off campus. You need to create a pictorial presentation that highlights a trip to a different country. Create a presentation using your own pictures. If you don't have access to any appropriate pictures, use the three pictures provided in the Data Files for this unit: PPT C-15.jpg, PPT C-16.jpg, and PPT C-17.jpg. *(NOTE: To complete steps below, your computer must be connected to the Internet.)*

a. Start PowerPoint, create a new blank presentation, and save it as **PPT C-Club** to the location where you store your Data Files.

b. Locate and insert the pictures you want to use. Place one picture on each slide using the Content with Caption slide layout.

c. Click the Crop list arrow, and use one of the other cropping options to crop a picture.

d. Add information about each picture in the text placeholder, and enter a slide title. If you use the pictures provided, research Truro, England, using the Internet for relevant information to place on the slides.

FIGURE C-21

e. Apply an appropriate design theme, then apply an appropriate title and your name to the title slide.

f. View the final presentation slide show (refer to **FIGURE C-21**).

g. Add a slide number and your class name as footer text to all of the slides, save your work, then submit your presentation to your instructor.

h. Close the file, and exit PowerPoint.

Visual Workshop

Create a one-slide presentation that looks like FIGURE C-22. The slide layout shown in FIGURE C-22 is a specific layout designed for pictures. Insert the picture file PPT C-18.jpg to complete this presentation. Add your name as footer text to the slide, save the presentation as **PPT C-Alaska** to the location where you store your Data Files, then submit your presentation to your instructor.

FIGURE C-22

Finishing a Presentation

CASE You have reviewed your work and are pleased with the slides you created for the Quest Specialty Travel presentation. Now you are ready to add some final touches and effects to the slides to make the PowerPoint presentation interesting to watch.

Unit Objectives

After completing this unit, you will be able to:

- Modify masters
- Customize the background and theme
- Use slide show commands
- Set slide transitions and timings

- Animate objects
- Use proofing and language tools
- Inspect a presentation
- Evaluate a presentation

Files You Will Need

PPT D-1.pptx   PPT D-6.pptx
PPT D-2.jpg   PPT D-7.jpg
PPT D-3.jpg   PPT D-8.pptx
PPT D-4.pptx   PPT D-9.pptx
PPT D-5.jpg

Modify Masters

Each presentation in PowerPoint has a set of **masters** that store information about the theme and slide layouts. Masters determine the position and size of text and content placeholders, fonts, slide background, color, and effects. There are three Master views: Slide Master view, Notes Master view, and Handout Master view. Changes made in Slide Master view are reflected on the slides in Normal view; changes made in Notes Master view are reflected in Notes Page view, and changes made in Handout Master view appear when you print your presentation using a handout printing option. The primary benefit to modifying a master is that you can make universal changes to your whole presentation instead of making individual repetitive changes to each of your slides. **CASE** ▶ *You want to add the QST company logo to every slide in your presentation, so you open your presentation and insert the logo to the slide master.*

STEPS

1. **Start PowerPoint, open the presentation PPT D-1.pptx from the location where you store your Data Files, save the presentation as PPT D-QST, then click the VIEW tab on the Ribbon**

   The title slide for the presentation appears.

2. **Click the Slide Master button in the Master Views group, scroll to the top of the Master Thumbnails pane, then click the Organic Slide Master thumbnail (first thumbnail)**

   The Slide Master view appears with the slide master displayed in the Slide pane as shown in **FIGURE D-1**. A new tab, the SLIDE MASTER tab, appears next to the HOME tab on the Ribbon. The slide master is the Organic theme slide master. Each theme comes with its own slide master. Each master text placeholder on the slide master identifies the font size, style, color, and position of text placeholders on the slides in Normal view. For example, for the Organic theme, the Master title placeholder positioned at the top of the slide uses a black, 44 pt, Garamond font. Slide titles use this font style and formatting. Each slide master comes with associated slide layouts located below the slide master in the Master Thumbnails pane. Slide layouts follow the information on the slide master, and changes you make are reflected in all of the slide layouts.

3. **Point to each of the slide layouts in the Master Thumbnails pane, then click the Title and Content Layout thumbnail**

   As you point to each slide layout, a ScreenTip appears identifying each slide layout by name and lists if any slides in the presentation are using the layout. Slides 2–6, and 13 are using the Title and Content Layout.

4. **Click the Organic Slide Master thumbnail, click the INSERT tab on the Ribbon, then click the Pictures button in the Images group**

   The Insert Picture dialog box opens.

5. **Select the picture file PPT D-2.jpg from the location where you store your Data Files, then click Insert**

   The QST logo picture is placed on the slide master and will now appear on all slides in the presentation. The picture is too large and needs to be repositioned on the slide.

6. **Click 1.61" in the Shape Width text box in the Size group, type .50, press [Enter], drag the QST logo to the upper-left corner of the slide, then click a blank area of the slide**

   The picture snaps into the corner of the slide.

7. **Click the SLIDE MASTER tab on the Ribbon, then click the Preserve button in the Edit Master group**

   Preserving the selected master ensures the Organic slide master remains with this presentation even if you eventually select another master. Compare your screen to **FIGURE D-2**.

8. **Click the Normal button 🖬 on the status bar, then save your changes**

FIGURE D-1: Slide Master view

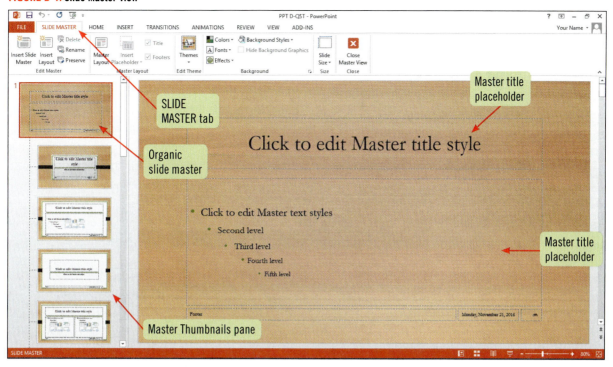

FIGURE D-2: Picture added to slide master

Create custom slide layouts

As you work with PowerPoint, you may find that you need to develop a customized slide layout. For example, you may need to create presentations for a client that has slides that display four pictures with a caption underneath each picture. To make everyone's job easier, you can create a custom slide layout that includes only the placeholders you need. To create a custom slide layout, open Slide Master view, and then click the Insert Layout button in the Edit Master group. A new slide layout appears below the last layout for the selected master in the slide thumbnails pane.

You can choose to add several different placeholders including Content, Text, Picture, Chart, Table, SmartArt, Media, and Picture. Click the Insert Placeholder list arrow in the Master Layout group, click the placeholder you want to add, drag + to create the placeholder, then position the placeholder on the slide. In Slide Master view, you can add or delete placeholders in any of the slide layouts. You can rename a custom slide layout by clicking the Rename button in the Edit Master group and entering a descriptive name to better identify the layout.

Customize the Background and Theme

Learning Outcomes
• Apply a slide background and change the style
• Modify presentation theme

Every slide in a PowerPoint presentation has a **background**, the area behind the text and graphics. You modify the background to enhance the slides using images and color. A **background graphic** is an object placed on the slide master. You can quickly change the background appearance by applying a background style, which is a set of color variations derived from the theme colors. Theme colors determine the colors for all slide elements in your presentation, including slide background, text and lines, shadows, fills, accents, and hyperlinks. Every PowerPoint theme has its own set of theme colors. See **TABLE D-1** for a description of the theme colors. **CASE ▶** *The QST presentation can be improved with some design enhancements. You decide to modify the background of the slides by changing the theme colors and fonts.*

STEPS

1. **Click the DESIGN tab on the Ribbon, then click the Format Background button in the Customize group**
   The Format Background pane opens displaying the Fill options. The Picture or texture fill option button is selected indicating the slide has a texture background.

2. **Click the Solid fill option button, review the slide, click the Gradient fill option button, review the slide, click the Pattern fill option button, then click the Diagonal brick pattern (sixth row)**
   FIGURE D-3 shows the new background on Slide 1 of the presentation. The new background style does not appear over the whole slide because there are background items on the slide master preventing you from seeing the entire slide background.

3. **Click the Hide Background Graphics check box in the Format Background pane**
   All of the background items, which include the QST logo, the white box behind the text objects, and the colored shapes, are hidden from view, and only the text objects and slide number remain visible.

4. **Click the Hide Background Graphics check box, then click the Reset Background button at the bottom of the Format Background pane**
   All of the background items and the texture slide background appear again as specified by the theme.

5. **Click the File button under Insert picture from section in the Format Background pane, select the picture file PPT D-3.jpg from the location where you store your Data Files, then click Insert**
   The new picture fills the slide background behind the background items.

6. **Click the Slide 3 thumbnail in the Thumbnails pane, then point to the dark brown theme variant in the Variants group**
   Notice how the new theme variant changes the color of the shapes on the slide and the background texture. A **variant** is a custom variation of the applied theme, in this case the Organic theme. Theme variants are similar to the original theme, but they are made up of different complementary colors, slide backgrounds, such as textures and patterns, and background elements, such as shapes and pictures.

7. **Point to the other variants in the Variants group, click the third variant from the left, click the Format Background pane Close button ✕, then save your work**
   The new variant is applied to the slide master and to all the slides in the presentation, except Slide 1. The slide background on Slide 1 did not change because you have already applied a picture to the slide background. Compare your screen to **FIGURE D-4**.

FIGURE D-3: New background style applied

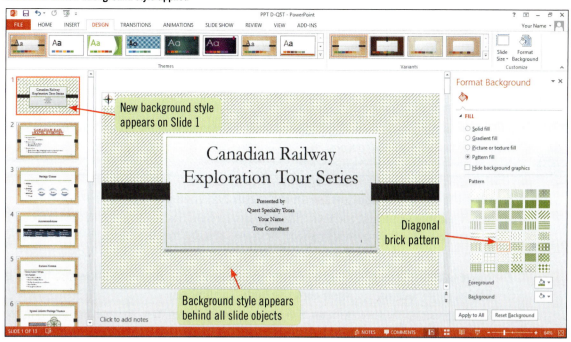

FIGURE D-4: New theme variant

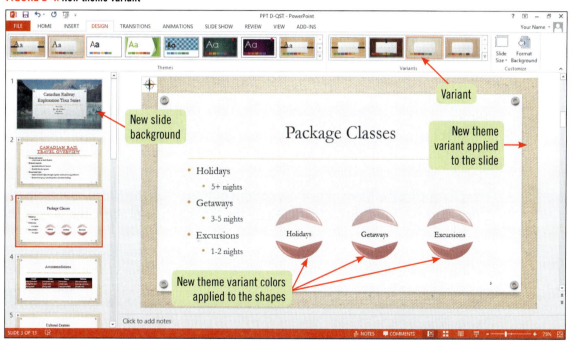

TABLE D-1: Theme colors

color element	description
Text/Background colors	Contrasting colors for typed characters and the slide background
Accent colors	There are six accent colors used for shapes, drawn lines, and text; the shadow color for text and objects and the fill and outline color for shapes are all accent colors; all of these colors contrast appropriately with background and text colors
Hyperlink color	Colors used for hyperlinks you insert
Followed Hyperlink color	Color used for hyperlinks after they have been clicked

Use Slide Show Commands

Learning Outcomes
• Preview a slide show
• Navigate a slide show
• Use slide show tools

With PowerPoint, Slide Show view is used primarily to deliver a presentation to an audience, either over the Internet using your computer or through a projector connected to your computer. As you've seen, Slide Show view fills your computer screen with the slides of the presentation, showing them one at a time. Once the presentation is in Slide Show view, you can draw, or **annotate**, on the slides or jump to other slides in the presentation.   **CASE** ▶ *You run the slide show of the presentation and practice using some of the custom slide show options.*

STEPS

1. **Click the Slide Show button 🖵 on the status bar, then press [Spacebar]**

   Slide 3 filled the screen first, and then Slide 4 appears. Pressing [Spacebar] or clicking the left mouse button is the easiest way to move through a slide show. See **TABLE D-2** for other basic slide show keyboard commands. You can easily navigate to other slides in the presentation during the slide show.

   TROUBLE
   The Slide Show toolbar buttons are semitransparent and blend in with the background color on the slide.

2. **Move ▷ to the lower-left corner of the screen to display the Slide Show toolbar, click the See all slides button ⊞, then click the Slide 1 thumbnail**

   Slide 1 appears on the screen with the Slide Show toolbar displayed. You can emphasize points in your presentation by annotating the slide during a slide show.

3. **Click the Pen and laser pointer tools button ⌀, on the Slide Show toolbar, then click Highlighter**

   The pointer changes to the highlighter pointer ▌. You can use the highlighter anywhere on the slide.

   QUICK TIP
   You can also use the Pen annotation tool to draw lines on a slide.

4. **Drag ▌, to highlight Presented by and Your Name in the subtitle text object, then press [Esc]**

   Two lines of text are highlighted as shown in **FIGURE D-5**. While the annotation tool is visible, mouse clicks do not advance the slide show; however, you can still move to the next slide by pressing [Spacebar] or [Enter]. Pressing [Esc] or [Ctrl][A] while using an annotation pointer switches the pointer back to ▷.

5. **Right-click anywhere on the screen, point to Pointer Options, click Eraser, the pointer changes to ⬚, then click the Your Name highlight annotation in the subtitle text object**

   The highlight annotation on the text is erased.

6. **Press [Esc], click the More slide show options button ⊙ on the Slide Show toolbar, click Show Presenter View, then click the Pause the timer button ‖ above the slide as shown in FIGURE D-6**

   Presenter view is a special view that you typically use when showing a presentation through two monitors; one that you see as the presenter and one that your audience sees. The current slide appears on the left of your screen (which is the only object your audience sees), the next slide in the presentation appears in the upper-right corner of the screen. Speaker notes, if you have any, appear in the lower-right corner. The timer you paused identifies how long the slide has been viewed by the audience.

7. **Click ⊙, click Hide Presenter View, then click the Advance to the next slide button ⊙ on the Slide Show toolbar**

   The next slide appears.

   QUICK TIP
   To temporarily hide your slide during a slide show, right-click the screen, point to Screen, then click Black Screen or White Screen.

8. **Press [Enter] to advance through the entire slide show until you see a black slide, then press [Spacebar]**

   If there are annotations on your slides, you have the option of saving them when you quit the slide show. Saved annotations appear as drawn objects in Normal view.

9. **Click Discard, then save the presentation**

   The highlight annotation is deleted on Slide 1, and Slide 3 appears in Normal view.

FIGURE D-5: Slide 1 in Slide Show view with annotations

FIGURE D-6: Slide 1 in Presenter view

TABLE D-2: Basic Slide Show view keyboard commands

keyboard commands	description
[Enter], [Spacebar], [PgDn], [N], [down arrow], or [right arrow]	Advances to the next slide
[E]	Erases the annotation drawing
[Home], [End]	Moves to the first or last slide in the slide show
[up arrow], [PgUp], or [left arrow]	Returns to the previous slide
[S]	Pauses the slide show when using automatic timings; press again to continue
[B]	Changes the screen to black; press again to return
[Esc]	Stops the slide show

Finishing a Presentation

Set Slide Transitions and Timings

In a slide show, you can determine how each slide advances in and out of view and how long each slide appears on the screen. **Slide transitions** are the special visual and audio effects you apply to a slide that determine how each slide moves on and off the screen during the slide show. **Slide timing** refers to the amount of time a slide is visible on the screen. Typically, you set slide timings only if you want the presentation to automatically progress through the slides during a slide show. Setting the correct slide timing, in this case, is important because it determines how much time your audience has to view each slide. Each slide can have a different slide transition and different slide timing. **CASE** *You decide to set slide transitions and 8-second slide timings for all the slides.*

STEPS

1. **Click the Slide 1 thumbnail in the Thumbnails pane, then click the TRANSITIONS tab on the Ribbon**

    Transitions are organized by type into three groups.

2. **Click the More button ▼ in the Transition to This Slide group, then click Blinds in the Exciting section**

    The new slide transition plays on the slide, and a transition icon ⭐ appears next to the slide thumbnail in the Thumbnails pane as shown in **FIGURE D-7**. You can customize the slide transition by changing its direction and speed.

3. **Click the Effect Options button in the Transition to This Slide group, click Horizontal, click the Duration up arrow in the Timing group until 2.00 appears, then click the Preview button in the Preview group**

    The Blinds slide transition now plays horizontal on the slide for 2.00 seconds. You can apply this transition with the custom settings to all of the slides in the presentation.

4. **Click the Apply To All button in the Timing group, then click the Slide Sorter button ▦ on the status bar**

    All of the slides now have the customized Blinds transition applied to them as identified by the transition icons located below each slide. You also have the ability to determine how slides progress during a slide show—either manually by mouse click or automatically by slide timing.

5. **Click the On Mouse Click check box under Advance Slide in the Timing group to clear the check mark**

    When this option is selected, you have to click to manually advance slides during a slide show. Now, with this option disabled, you can set the slides to advance automatically after a specified amount of time.

6. **Click the After up arrow in the Timing group, until 00:08.00 appears in the text box, then click the Apply To All button**

    The timing between slides is 8 seconds as indicated by the time under each slide in Slide Sorter view. See **FIGURE D-8**. When you run the slide show, each slide will remain on the screen for 8 seconds. You can override a slide's timing and speed up the slide show by clicking the left mouse button.

7. **Click the Slide Show button 🖵 on the status bar**

    The slide show advances automatically. A new slide appears every 8 seconds using the Blinds transition.

8. **When you see the black slide, press [Spacebar], then save your changes**

    The slide show ends and returns to Slide Sorter view with Slide 1 selected.

FIGURE D-7: Applied slide transition

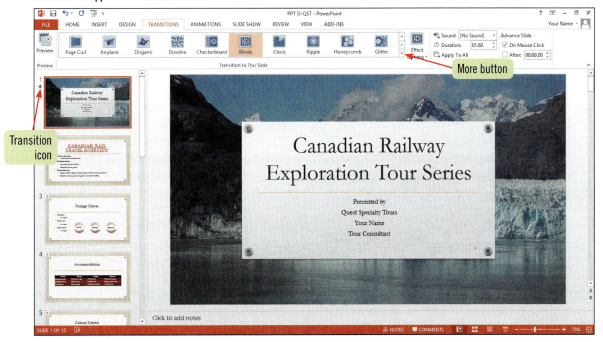

FIGURE D-8: Slide sorter view showing applied transition and timing

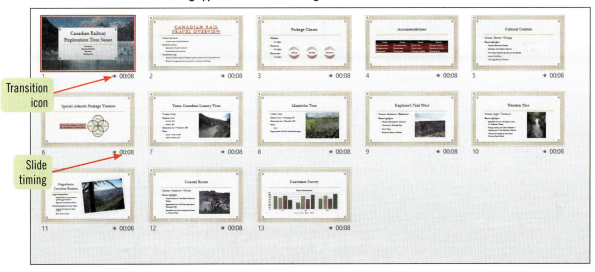

Rehearsing slide show timings

You can set different slide timings for each slide; for example, the title slide can appear for 20 seconds and the second slide for 1 minute. To set timings click the Rehearse Timings button in the Set Up group on the SLIDE SHOW tab. Slide Show view opens and the Recording toolbar shown in **FIGURE D-9** opens. It contains buttons to pause between slides and to advance to the next slide. After opening the Recording toolbar, you can practice giving your presentation by manually advancing each slide in the presentation. When you are finished, PowerPoint displays the total recorded time for the presentation and you have the option to save the recorded timings. The next time you run the slide show, you can use the timings you rehearsed.

FIGURE D-9: Recording toolbar

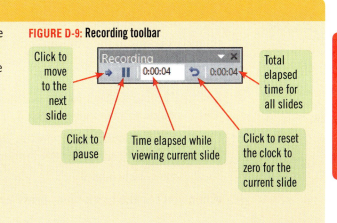

Animate Objects

Animations let you control how objects and text appear and move on the screen during a slide show and allow you to manage the flow of information and emphasize specific facts. You can animate text, pictures, sounds, hyperlinks, SmartArt diagrams, charts, and individual chart elements. For example, you can apply a Fade animation to bulleted text so each paragraph enters the slide separately from the others. Animations are organized into four categories, Entrance, Emphasis, Exit, and Motion Paths. The Entrance and Exit animations cause an object to enter or exit the slide with an effect. An Emphasis animation causes an object visible on the slide to have an effect and a Motion Path animation causes an object to move on a specified path on the slide. **CASE** ▶ *You animate the text and graphics of several slides in the presentation.*

STEPS

1. **Double-click the Slide 3 thumbnail to return to Normal view, click the ANIMATIONS tab on the Ribbon, then click the circle shapes object**

   Text as well as other objects, like a picture, can be animated during a slide show.

   QUICK TIP
   There are additional animation options for each animation category located at the bottom of the animations gallery.

2. **Click the More button ▾ in the Animation group, then click Spin in the Emphasis section**

   Animations can be serious and business-like, or humorous, so be sure to choose appropriate effects for your presentation. A small numeral 1, called an animation tag ▢, appears at the top corner of the object. **Animation tags** identify the order in which objects are animated during slide show.

3. **Click the Effect Options button in the Animation group, click Two Spins, then click the Duration up arrow in the Timing group until 03.00 appears**

   Effect options are different for every animation, and some animations don't have effect options. Changing the animation timing increases the duration of the animation and gives it a more dramatic effect. Compare your screen to **FIGURE D-10**.

4. **Click the Slide Show button 🖵 on the status bar until you see Slide 4, then press [Esc]**

   After the slide transition finishes, the shapes object spins twice for a total of three seconds.

5. **Click the Slide 2 thumbnail in the Thumbnails pane, click the bulleted list text object, then click Float In in the Animation group**

   The text object is animated with the Float In animation. Each line of text has an animation tag with each paragraph displaying a different number. Accordingly, each paragraph is animated separately.

6. **Click the Effect Options button in the Animation group, click All at Once, click the Duration up arrow in the Timing group until 02.50 appears, then click the Preview button in the Preview group**

   Notice the animation tags for each line of text in the text object now have the same numeral (1), indicating that each line of text animates at the same time.

   QUICK TIP
   If you want to individually animate the parts of a grouped object, then you must ungroup the objects before you animate them.

7. **Click Canadian in the title text object, click ▾ in the Animation group, scroll down, then click Loops in the Motion Paths section**

   A motion path object appears over the shapes object and identifies the direction and shape, or path, of the animation. When needed, you can move, resize, and change the direction of the motion path. Notice the numeral 2 animation tag next to the title text object indicating it is animated *after* the bulleted list text object. Compare your screen to **FIGURE D-11**.

8. **Click the Move Earlier button in the Timing group, click the SLIDE SHOW tab on the Ribbon, then click the From Beginning button in the Start Slide Show group**

   The slide show begins from Slide 1. The animations make the presentation more interesting to view.

9. **When you see the black slide, press [Enter], then save your changes**

FIGURE D-10: Animation applied to shape object

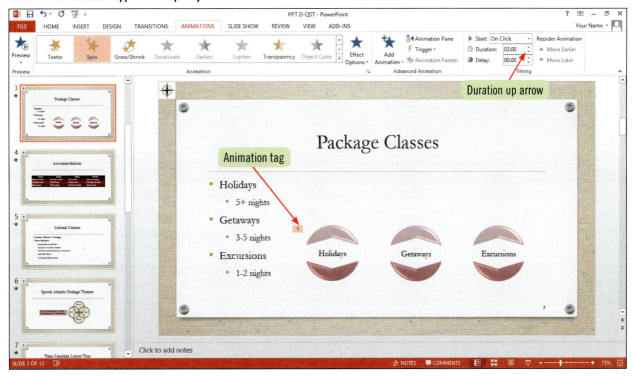

FIGURE D-11: Motion path applied to text object

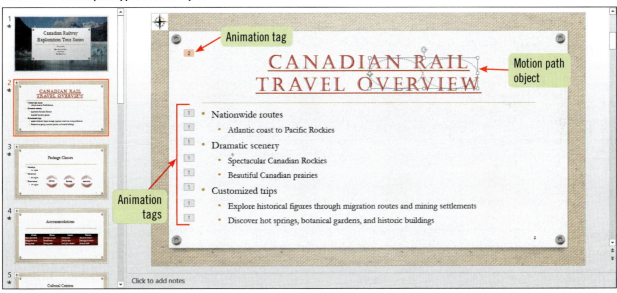

Attaching a sound to an animation

Text or objects that have animation applied can be customized further by attaching a sound for extra emphasis. First, select the animated object, then on the ANIMATIONS tab click the Animation Pane button in the Advanced Animation group. In the Animation Pane, click the animation you want to apply the sound to, click the Animation list arrow, then click Effect Options to open the animation effect's dialog box. In the Enhancements section, click the Sound list arrow, then choose a sound. Click OK when you are finished. Now, when you run the slide show, the sound you applied will play with the animation.

Finishing a Presentation

Use Proofing and Language Tools

Learning Outcomes
• Spell check a presentation
• Translate slide text

As your work on the presentation file nears completion, you need to review and proofread your slides thoroughly for errors. You can use the Spell Checker feature in PowerPoint to check for and correct spelling errors. This feature compares the spelling of all the words in your presentation against the words contained in the dictionary. You still must proofread your presentation for punctuation, grammar, and word-usage errors because the Spell Checker recognizes only misspelled and unknown words, not misused words. For example, the spell checker would not identify the word "last" as an error, even if you had intended to type the word "cast." PowerPoint also includes language tools that translate words or phrases from your default language into another language using the Microsoft Translator. **CASE** *You're finished working on the presentation for now, so it's a good time to check spelling. You then experiment with language translation because the final presentation will be translated into French.*

STEPS

1. **Click the REVIEW tab on the Ribbon, then click the Spelling button in the Proofing group**

   PowerPoint begins to check the spelling in your presentation. When PowerPoint finds a misspelled word or a word that is not in its dictionary, the Spelling pane opens, as shown in **FIGURE D-12**. In this case, PowerPoint identifies the misspelled word in the table on Slide 4 and suggests you replace it with the correctly spelled word "Business."

2. **Click Change in the Spelling pane**

   PowerPoint changes the misspelled word and then continues to check the rest of the presentation for errors. This presentation has several names that are not in the dictionary that you can ignore. If PowerPoint finds any other words it does not recognize, either change or ignore them. When the Spell Checker finishes checking your presentation, the Spelling pane closes, and an alert box opens with a message stating the spelling check is complete.

3. **Click OK in the Alert box, then click the Slide 1 thumbnail in the Thumbnails pane**

   The alert box closes. Now you need to see how the language translation feature works.

4. **Click the Translate button in the Language group, then click Choose Translation Language**

   The Translation Language Options dialog box opens.

5. **Click the Translate to list arrow, click Hebrew, then click OK**

   The Translation Language Options dialog box closes.

6. **Click the Translate button in the Language group, click Mini Translator [Hebrew], click anywhere in the subtitle text object, then select all of the text**

   The Microsoft Translator begins to analyze the selected text, and a semitransparent Microsoft Translator box appears below the text. The Mini toolbar may also appear.

7. **Move the pointer over the Microsoft Translator box**

   A Hebrew translation of the text appears as shown in **FIGURE D-13**. The translation language setting remains in effect until you reset it.

8. **Click the Translate button in the Language group, click Choose Translation Language, click the Translate to list arrow, click Arabic, click OK, click the Translate button again, then click Mini Translator [Arabic]**

   The Mini Translator is turned off, and the translation language is restored to the default setting.

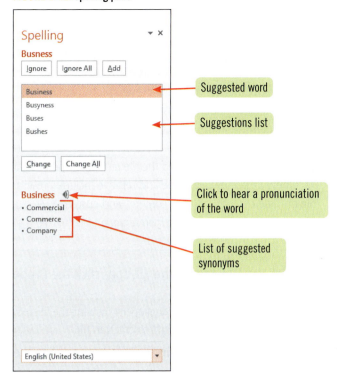

Suggested word

Suggestions list

Click to hear a pronunciation of the word

List of suggested synonyms

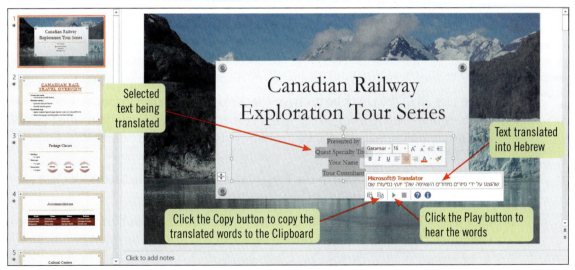

Selected text being translated

Text translated into Hebrew

Click the Copy button to copy the translated words to the Clipboard

Click the Play button to hear the words

Checking spelling as you type

By default, PowerPoint checks your spelling as you type. If you type a word that is not in the dictionary, a wavy red line appears under it. To correct an error, right-click the misspelled word, then review the suggestions, which appear in the shortcut menu. You can select a suggestion, add the word you typed to your custom dictionary, or ignore it. To turn off automatic spell checking, click the FILE tab, then click Options to open the PowerPoint Options dialog box. Click Proofing in the left column, then click the Check spelling as you type check box to deselect it. To temporarily hide the wavy red lines, click the Hide spelling errors check box to select it. Contextual spelling in PowerPoint identifies common grammatically misused words, for example, if you type the word "their" and the correct word is "there," PowerPoint will identify the mistake and place a wavy red line under the word. To turn contextual spelling on or off, click Proofing in the PowerPoint Options dialog box, then click the Check grammar with spelling check box.

Inspect a Presentation

Learning Outcomes
• Modify document properties
• Inspect and remove unwanted data

Reviewing your presentation can be an important step. You should not only find and fix errors, but also locate and delete confidential company or personal information and document properties you do not want to share with others. If you share presentations with others, especially over the Internet, it is a good idea to inspect the presentation file using the Document Inspector. The **Document Inspector** looks for hidden data and personal information that is stored in the file itself or in the document properties. Document properties, also known as **metadata**, includes specific data about the presentation, such as the author's name, subject matter, title, who saved the file last, and when the file was created. Other types of information the Document Inspector can locate and remove include presentation notes, comments, ink annotations, invisible on-slide content, off-slide content, and custom XML data. **CASE** ▶ *You decide to view and add some document properties, inspect your presentation file, and learn about the Mark as Final command.*

STEPS

QUICK TIP
Click the Properties list button, then click Advanced Properties to open the Properties dialog box to see or change more document properties.

1. **Click the FILE tab on the Ribbon, click the Properties button, then click Show Document Panel**

   The Document Properties panel opens showing the file location and the title of the presentation. Now enter some descriptive data for this presentation file.

2. **Enter the data shown in FIGURE D-14, then click the Document Properties panel Close button** ✕

   This data provides detailed information about the presentation file that you can use to identify and organize your file. You can also use this information as search criteria to locate the file at a later time. You now use the Document Inspector to search for information you might want to delete in the presentation.

QUICK TIP
If you need to save a presentation to run in an earlier version of PowerPoint, check for unsupported features using the Check Compatibility feature.

3. **Click the FILE tab on the Ribbon, click the Check for Issues button, click Inspect Document, then click Yes to save the changes to the document**

   The Document Inspector dialog box opens. The Document Inspector searches the presentation file for seven different types of information that you might want removed from the presentation before sharing it.

4. **Make sure all of the check boxes have check marks, then click Inspect**

   The presentation file is reviewed, and the results are shown in **FIGURE D-15**. The Document Inspector found items having to do with document properties, which you just entered, and presentation notes, which are on Slide 13. You decide to leave the document properties alone but delete the notes.

5. **Click the Remove All button in the Presentation Notes section, then click Close**

   All notes are removed from the Notes pane for the slides in the presentation.

6. **Click the FILE tab on the Ribbon, click the Protect Presentation button, click Mark as Final, then click OK in the alert box**

   An information alert box opens. Be sure to read the message to understand what happens to the file and how to recognize a marked-as-final presentation. You decide to complete this procedure.

7. **Click OK, click the HOME tab on the Ribbon, then click anywhere in the title text object**

   When you select the title text object, the Ribbon closes automatically and an information alert box at the top of the window notes that the presentation is marked as final, making it a read-only file. Compare your screen to **FIGURE D-16**. A **read-only** file is one that can't be edited or modified in any way. Anyone who has received a read-only presentation can only edit the presentation by changing its marked-as-final status. You still want to work on the presentation, so you remove the marked-as-final status.

8. **Click the Edit Anyway button in the information alert box, then save your changes**

   The Ribbon and all commands are active again, and the file can now be modified.

FIGURE D-15: Document Inspector dialog box

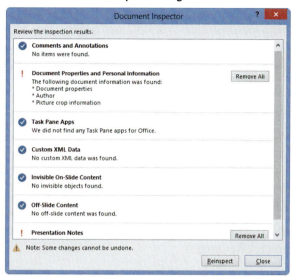

FIGURE D-16: Marked As Final presentation

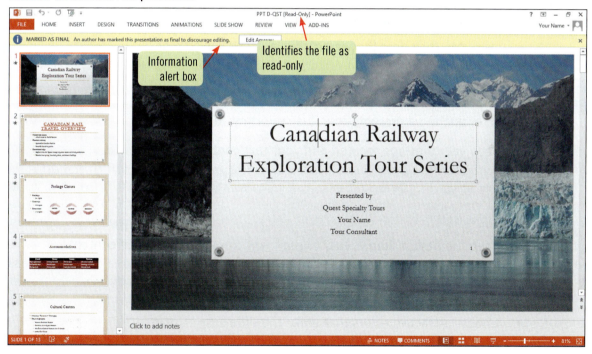

Digitally sign a presentation

What is a digital signature, and why would you want to use one in PowerPoint? A **digital signature** is similar to a handwritten signature in that it authenticates your document; however, a digital signature, unlike a handwritten signature, is created using computer cryptography and is not visible within the presentation itself. There are three primary reasons you would add a digital signature to a presentation: one, to authenticate the signer of the document; two, to ensure that the content of the presentation has not been changed since it was signed; and three, to assure the reader of the origin of the signed document. To add a digital signature, click the FILE tab on the Ribbon, click the Protect Presentation button, click Add a Digital Signature, then follow the dialog boxes.

Evaluate a Presentation

A well-designed and organized presentation requires thought and preparation. An effective presentation is focused and visually appealing—easy for the speaker to present, and simple for the audience to understand. Visual elements can strongly influence the audience's attention and can influence the success of your presentation. **CASE** *You know your boss and other colleagues will critique your presentation, so you take the time to evaluate your presentation's organization and effectiveness.*

STEPS

1. **Click the Reading View button 📖 on the status bar, then press [Spacebar] when the slide show finishes**

> **QUICK TIP**
> You can also move, delete, collapse, and expand a section in the Thumbnails tab or in Slide Sorter view.

2. **Click the Slide 5 thumbnail in the Thumbnails pane, click the Section button in the Slides group, then click Add Section**

   The presentation is divided into two sections, which appear in the Thumbnails pane. The section you created is the Untitled Section, and the section for all the slides before the new section is the Default Section. Sections help you organize your slides into logical groups.

3. **Right-click Untitled Section in the Thumbnails pane, click Rename Section, type Tour Packages, then click Rename**

4. **Click the Slide Sorter view button ⊞ on the status bar, save your work, then compare your screen to FIGURE D-17**

5. **Double-click Slide 1, add your name to the notes and handouts footer, evaluate your presentation according to the guidelines below, submit your presentation to your instructor, then close the presentation and exit PowerPoint**

   FIGURE D-18 shows a poorly designed slide. Contrast this slide with the guidelines below and your presentation.

DETAILS

When evaluating a presentation, it is important to:

• **Keep your message focused and your text concise**

   Don't put every word you plan to say on your slides. Your presentation text should only provide highlights of your message. Keep the audience anticipating explanations to the key points in the presentation. Supplement the information on your slides with further explanation and details during your presentation. Try to limit each slide to six words per line and six lines per slide. Use bulleted lists to help prioritize your points visually.

• **Keep the design simple, easy to read, and appropriate for the content**

   A design theme makes the presentation visually consistent. If you design your own layout, use similar design elements and limit the number of design elements, using them sparingly throughout the presentation; otherwise, your audience may get overwhelmed and not understand the message.

• **Choose attractive colors that make the slide easy to read**

   Use contrasting complementary colors for slide background and text to make the text readable.

• **Choose fonts and styles that are easy to read and emphasize important text**

   As a general rule, use no more than two fonts in a presentation and vary the font size. If you are giving an on-screen presentation, use nothing smaller than 24 points. Use bold and italic attributes selectively.

• **Use visuals to help communicate the message of your presentation**

   Commonly used visuals include clip art, photographs, charts, worksheets, tables, and videos. Whenever possible, replace text with a visual, but be careful not to overcrowd your slides. White space on your slides enhances the presentation.

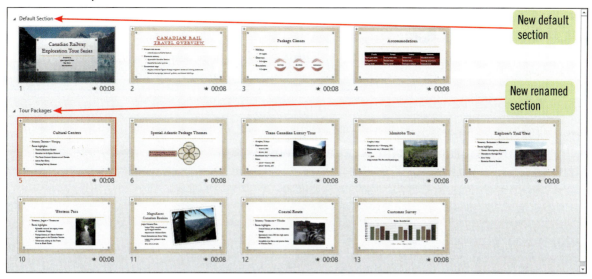

FIGURE D-18: A poorly designed slide

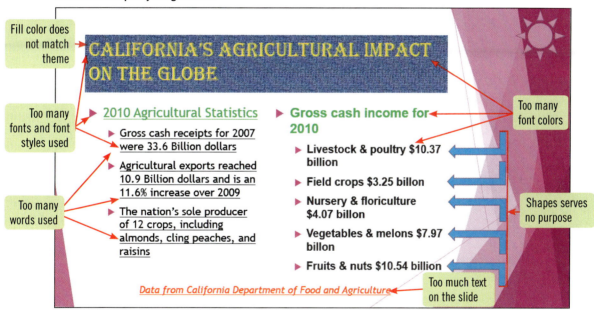

Setting permissions

In PowerPoint, you can set specific access permissions for people who review or edit your work so you have better control over your content. For example, you may want to give a user permission to edit or change your presentation but not allow them to print it. You can also restrict a user by permitting them to view the presentation without the ability to edit or print the presentation, or you can give the user full access or control of the presentation. To use this feature, you first must have access to an information rights management service from Microsoft or another rights management company. Then, to set user access permissions, click the FILE tab, click the Protect Presentation button, point to Restrict Access, then click an appropriate option.

PowerPoint 2013

Practice

Concepts Review

Label each element of the PowerPoint window shown in FIGURE D-19.

FIGURE D-19

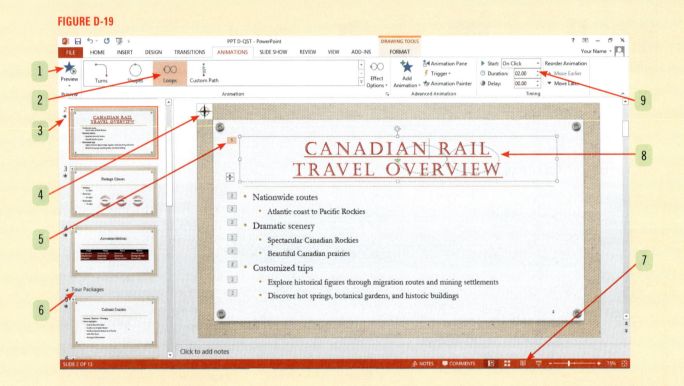

Match each term with the statement that best describes it.

10. **Transitions**
11. **Exception**
12. **Background graphic**
13. **Annotate**
14. **Masters**
15. **Animations**

a. An object placed on the slide master
b. Slides that store theme and placeholder information
c. Visual effects that determine how objects appears on the slide
d. Visual effects that determine how a slide moves in and out of view during a slide show
e. A change you make to a slide that does not follow the theme
f. To draw on a slide during a slide show

Select the best answer from the list of choices.

16. The Document Inspector looks for _____ and personal information that is stored in the presentation file.
    - **a.** Themes
    - **b.** Hidden data
    - **c.** Animation tags
    - **d.** Video settings

17. Apply a(n) _____ to your presentation to quickly modify the applied theme.
    - **a.** Variant
    - **b.** Exception
    - **c.** Theme
    - **d.** Animation

18. Which PowerPoint file *can't* be edited or modified?
    - **a.** Inspected file
    - **b.** File saved in another file format
    - **c.** Read-only file
    - **d.** Template file

19. Use _____ view to show your presentation through two monitors.
    - **a.** Reading
    - **b.** Presenter
    - **c.** Slide Show
    - **d.** Projector

20. Set slide _____ to make your presentation automatically progress through the slides during a slide show.
    - **a.** Animations
    - **b.** Autoplay effects
    - **c.** Variants
    - **d.** Timings

21. According to the book, which guidelines should you follow when you create a presentation?
    - **a.** Slides should include most of the information you wish to present.
    - **b.** Use many different design elements to keep your audience from getting bored.
    - **c.** Slides should outline the message in a concise way.
    - **d.** Use text rather than visuals as often as possible.

22. Which of the following statements about masters is *not* true?
    - **a.** Changes made to the slide master are reflected in the handout and notes masters as well.
    - **b.** Masters store information.
    - **c.** Each slide layout in the presentation has a corresponding slide layout in Slide Master view.
    - **d.** The design theme is placed on the slide master.

Skills Review

1. **Modify masters.**
   - **a.** Open the presentation PPT D-4.pptx from the location where you store your Data Files, then save the presentation as **PPT D-DataSource**.
   - **b.** Open Slide Master view using the VIEW tab, then click the Integral Slide Master thumbnail.
   - **c.** Insert the picture PPT D-5.jpg, then resize the picture so it is 1.0" wide.
   - **d.** Drag the picture to the upper-right corner of the slide within the design frame of the slide, then deselect the picture.
   - **e.** Preserve the Integral master, switch to Normal view, then save your changes.

2. **Customize the background and theme.**
   - **a.** Click the DESIGN tab, click the More button in the Variants group, then click the first variant in the second row.
   - **b.** Go to Slide 4, then open the Format Background pane.
   - **c.** Click the Color button, then click Tan, Accent 2 in the top row.
   - **d.** Set the Transparency to 50%, close the Format Background pane then save your changes.

Skills Review (continued)

3. **Use slide show commands.**
   a. Open Slide Show view, then go to Slide 1 using the See all slides button on the Slide Show toolbar.
   b. Use the Pen annotation tool to circle the slide title.
   c. Go to Slide 2, then use the Highlighter to highlight four points in the bulleted text on the slide.
   d. Erase two highlight annotations on the bulleted text, then press [Esc].
   e. Open Presenter view, then stop the timer.
   f. Advance the slides to Slide 5, then click the Zoom into the slide button (now called the Zoom out button) on the Slide Show toolbar, then click in the center of the graph.
   g. Click the Zoom into the slide button, then return to Slide 1.
   h. Hide Presenter view, advance through the slide show, don't save any ink annotations, then save your work.

4. **Set slide transitions and timings.**
   a. Go to Slide Sorter view, click the Slide 1 thumbnail, then apply the Ripple transition to the slide.
   b. Change the effect option to From Bottom-Right, change the duration speed to 2.50, then apply to all the slides.
   c. Change the slide timing to 5 seconds, then apply to all of the slides.
   d. Switch to Normal view, view the slide show, then save your work.

5. **Animate objects.**
   a. Go to Slide 3, click the ANIMATIONS tab, then select the double-headed arrow on the slide.
   b. Apply the Split effect to the object, click the Pricing shape, apply the Shape effect, then preview the animations.
   c. Click the COG shape, apply the Shape effect, then preview the animations.
   d. Select the Pricing shape and the COG shape, click the Effect Options button, then click Box.
   e. Click the double-headed arrow, click the Effect Options button, click Horizontal Out, then preview the animations.

6. **Use proofing and language tools.**
   a. Check the spelling of the document, and change any misspelled words. Ignore any words that are correctly spelled but that the spell checker doesn't recognize. There is one misspelled word in the presentation.
   b. Go to Slide 3, then set the Mini Translator language to Ukrainian.
   c. View the Ukrainian translation of text on Slide 3.
   d. Choose one other language (or as many as you want), translate words or phrases on the slide, reset the default language to Arabic, turn off the Mini Translator, then save your changes.

7. **Inspect a presentation.**
   a. Open the Document Properties pane, type your name in the Author text box, type **Internet Product** in the Subject text box, then type **Review** in the Status text box.
   b. Close the Document Properties pane, then open the Document Inspector dialog box.
   c. Make sure the Off-Slide Content check box is selected, then inspect the presentation.
   d. Delete the off-slide content, then close the dialog box. Save your changes.

8. **Evaluate a presentation.**
   a. Go to Slide 4, add a section, then rename it **Pricing and Sales**.
   b. Select the Default section at the top of the Thumbnails pane, then rename it **Intro**.
   c. Go to Slide 1, then run a slide show.
   d. Evaluate the presentation using the points described in the lesson as criteria, then submit a written evaluation to your instructor.
   e. Add the slide number and your name to the slide footer on all the slides, then save your changes.

Skills Review (continued)

f. Switch to Slide Sorter view, then compare your presentation to **FIGURE D-20**.

g. Submit your presentation to your instructor, then close the presentation.

FIGURE D-20

Independent Challenge 1

You are a travel consultant for Pacific Tour Enterprises, located in Houston, Texas. You have been working on a sales presentation that is going to be accessed by customers on the company Web site. You need to finish up what you have been working on by adding transitions, timings, and animation effects to the sales presentation.

a. Open the file PPT D-6.pptx from the location where you store your Data Files, and save the presentation as **PPT D-Pacific**.

b. Add the slide number and your name as the footer on all slides, except the title slide.

c. Open Slide Master View, click the Facet Slide Master thumbnail, insert the picture PPT D-7.jpg, then resize the picture so it is 1.0" wide.

d. Right-click a blank area of the master slide, point to Grid and Guides, click Add Vertical Guide, then make sure the guide is in the center of the master slide.

e. Move the picture to the top of the slide centered over the vertical guide, remove the vertical guide, then close Slide Master view.

f. Apply the Wipe animation to the title text on each slide.

g. Apply the Underline animation to the bulleted text objects on each slide.

h. Apply the Shape animation to the table on Slide 5, then change the effect option to Box.

i. Apply the Comb slide transition, apply a 7-second slide timing, then apply to all of the slides.

j. Check the spelling of the presentation, then save your changes.

k. View the slide show, and evaluate your presentation. Make changes if necessary.

l. Submit your presentation to your instructor, close the presentation, then exit PowerPoint.

Independent Challenge 2

You are a development engineer at Advanced Performance Sports, Inc., an international sports product design company located in Phoenix, Arizona. Advanced Performance designs and manufactures items such as bike helmets, bike racks, and kayak paddles, and markets these items primarily to countries in North America and Western Europe. You need to finish the work on a quarterly presentation that outlines the progress of the company's newest technologies by adding animations, customizing the background, and using the Document Inspector.

a. Open the file PPT D-8.pptx from the location where you store your Data Files, and save the presentation as **PPT D-Sports**.

Independent Challenge 2 (continued)

b. Apply an appropriate design theme, then apply a gradient fill slide background to the title slide using the Format Background pane.

c. Apply the Glitter slide transition to all slides, then animate the following objects: the bulleted text on Slide 2 and the table on Slide 4. View the slide show to evaluate the effects you added and make adjustments as necessary.

d. Use the Microsoft Translator to translate the bulleted text on Slide 2 using two different languages.

e. Run the Document Inspector with all options selected, identify what items the Document Inspector finds, close the Document Inspector dialog box, then review the slides to find the items.

f. Add a slide at the end of the presentation that identifies the items the Document Inspector found.

g. Run the Document Inspector again, and remove all items except the document properties.

h. View the slide show, and make annotations to the slides. Save the annotations at the end of the slide show.

i. Add your name as a footer to all slides, run the spell checker, save your work, then run the slide show to evaluate your presentation.

j. Submit your presentation to your instructor, then close the presentation and exit PowerPoint.

Independent Challenge 3

You work for Thomas Lincoln & Associates, a full-service investment and pension firm. Your manager wants you to create a presentation on small business pension plan options. You have completed adding the information to the presentation, now you need to add a design theme, format information to highlight certain facts, add animation effects, and add slide timings.

a. Open the file PPT D-9.pptx from the location where you store your Data Files, and save the presentation as **PPT D-Thomas**.

b. Apply an appropriate design theme, then apply a theme variant.

c. Apply animation effects to the following objects: the shapes on Slide 3 and the bulleted text on Slide 5. View the slide show to evaluate the effects you added, and make adjustments as necessary.

d. Convert the text on Slide 4 to a Radial Cycle SmartArt graphic (found in the Cycle category).

e. Apply the Polished Effect style to the SmartArt graphic.

f. Go to Slide 3, align the Sector and Quality arrow shapes to their bottoms, then align the Allocation and Maturity arrow shapes to their right edges.

g. On Slides 6 and 7 change the table style format to Light Style2 - Accent 4, and adjust the position of the tables on the slides, if necessary.

h. Apply a 10-second timing to Slides 3–7 and a 5-second timing to Slides 1 and 2.

i. Add a section between Slide 5 and Slide 6, then rename the section **Plans**.

j. Rename the Default section in the Slides tab to **Intro**.

k. Add your name as a footer to the slides, run the Spell Checker, save your work, then run the slide show to evaluate your presentation. An example of a finished presentation is shown in **FIGURE D-21**.

FIGURE D-21

l. Submit your presentation to your instructor, then close the presentation and exit PowerPoint.

Independent Challenge 4: Explore

You work for the operations supervisor at the Southern Alabama State University student union. Create a presentation that you can eventually publish to the college Web site that describes all of the services offered at the student union. (*Note: To complete this Independent Challenge, you may need to be connected to the Internet.*)

a. Plan and create the slide presentation that describes the services and events offered at the student union. To help create content, use the student union at your school or use the Internet to locate information on college student unions. The presentation should contain at least six slides.

b. Use an appropriate design theme.

c. Add at least one photograph to the presentation, then style and customize one photo.

d. Save the presentation as **PPT D-SASU** to the location where you store your Data Files. View the slide show, and evaluate the contents of your presentation. Make any necessary adjustments.

e. Add slide transitions and animation effects to the presentation. View the slide show again to evaluate the effects you added.

f. To help you to complete this step, use the information on rehearsing slide timings found in the Set Slide Transition and Timings lesson in this unit. Click the Slide Show tab, click the Rehearse Timings button in the Set Up group, then click the Next button on the Recording toolbar to advance each slide in the presentation.

g. Click Yes to save slides timings at the end of the slide show.

h. Go to Slide 2, translate the bottom text box into Korean, then click the Copy button on the Microsoft Translator box.

i. Insert a new text box on Slide 2, paste the Korean text into the text box, then move the Korean text box below the translated English text box.

j. Change the language in the Microsoft translator back to Arabic, then turn off the Microsoft Translator.

k. Add the slide number and your name as a footer to the slides, check the spelling, inspect, then save the presentation.

l. Submit your presentation to your instructor, then exit PowerPoint. An example of a finished presentation is shown in **FIGURE D-22**.

FIGURE D-22

Visual Workshop

Create a one-slide presentation that looks like FIGURE D-23, which shows a slide with a specific slide layout, slide background, theme, and theme variant. Add your name as footer text to the slide, save the presentation as **PPT D-Glacier** to the location where you store your Data Files, then submit your presentation to your instructor.

FIGURE D-23

Working in the Cloud

CASE ▶ In your job for the Vancouver branch of Quest Specialty Travel, you travel frequently, you often work from home, and you also collaborate online with colleagues and clients. You want to learn how you can use SkyDrive with Office 2013 to work in the Cloud so that you can access and work on your files anytime and anywhere. (*Note*: SkyDrive and Office Web Apps are dynamic Web pages, and might change over time, including the way they are organized and how commands are performed. The steps and figures in this appendix reflect these pages at the time this book was published.)

Unit Objectives

After completing this unit, you will be able to:

- Understand Office 2013 in the Cloud
- Work Online
- Explore SkyDrive
- Manage Files on SkyDrive

- Share Files
- Explore Office Web Apps
- Complete a Team Project

Files You Will Need

WEB-1.pptx
WEB-2.docx

Understand Office 2013 in the Cloud

The term **cloud computing** refers to the process of working with files and apps online. You may already be familiar with Web-based e-mail accounts such as Gmail and outlook.com. These applications are **cloud-based**, which means that you do not need a program installed on your computer to run them. Office 2013 has also been designed as a cloud-based application. When you work in Office 2013, you can choose to store your files "in the cloud" so that you can access them on any device connected to the Internet. **CASE** *You review the concepts related to working online with Office 2013.*

DETAILS

• ### How does Office 2013 work in the Cloud?

When you launch an Office application such as Word or Excel, you might see your name and maybe even your picture in the top right corner of your screen. This information tells you that you have signed in to Office 2013, either with your personal account or with an account you are given as part of an organization such as a company or school. When you are signed in to Office and click the FILE tab in any Office 2013 application such as Word or Excel, you see a list of the files that you have used recently on your current computer and on any other connected device such as a laptop, a tablet or even a Windows phone. The file path appears beneath each filename so that you can quickly identify its location as shown in **FIGURE WEB-1**. Office 2013 also remembers your personalized settings so that they are available on all the devices you use.

• ### What are roaming settings?

A **roaming setting** is a setting that travels with you on every connected device. Examples of roaming settings include your personal settings such as your name and picture, the files you've used most recently, your list of connected services such as Facebook and Twitter, and any custom dictionaries you've created. Two particularly useful roaming settings are the Word Resume Reading Position setting and the PowerPoint Last Viewed Slide setting. For example, when you open a PowerPoint presentation that you've worked on previously, you will see a message similar to the one shown in **FIGURE WEB-2**.

• ### What is SkyDrive?

SkyDrive is an online storage and file sharing service. When you are signed in to your computer with your Microsoft account, you receive access to your own SkyDrive, which is your personal storage area on the Internet. On your SkyDrive, you are given space to store up to 7 GB of data online. A SkyDrive location is already created on your computer as shown in **FIGURE WEB-3**. Every file you save to SkyDrive is synced among your computers and your personal storage area on SkyDrive.com. The term **synced** (which stands for synchronized) means that when you add, change or delete files on one computer, the same files on your other devices are also updated.

• ### What are Office Web Apps?

Office Web Apps are versions of Microsoft Word, Excel, PowerPoint, and OneNote that you can access online from your SkyDrive. An Office Web App does not include all of the features and functions included with the full Office version of its associated application. However, you can use the Office Web App from any computer that is connected to the Internet, even if Microsoft Office 2013 is not installed on that computer.

• ### How do SkyDrive and Office Web Apps work together?

You can create a file in Office 2013 using Word, Excel, PowerPoint, or OneNote and then save it to your SkyDrive. You can then open the Office file saved to SkyDrive and edit it using your Office 2013 apps. If you do not have Office 2013 installed on the computer you are using, you can edit the file using your Web browser and the corresponding Office Web App. You can also use an Office Web App to create a new file, which is saved automatically to SkyDrive while you work and you can download a file created with an Office Web App and work with the file in the full version of the corresponding Office application.

FIGURE WEB-1: FILE tab in Microsoft Excel

FIGURE WEB-2: PowerPoint Last Viewed Slide setting

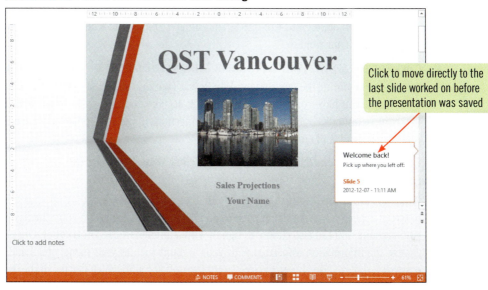

FIGURE WEB-3: Saving a Word file on SkyDrive

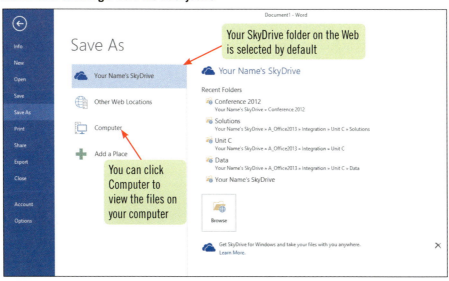

Work Online

When you work on your own computer, you are usually signed in to your Microsoft account automatically. When you use another person's computer or a public computer, you will be required to enter the password associated with your Microsoft account to access files you have saved on Windows SkyDrive. You know you are signed in to Windows when you see your name and possibly your picture in the top right corner of your screen. *Note*: To complete the steps below, you need to be signed in to your Microsoft account. If you do not have a Microsoft account, see "Getting a Microsoft account" in the yellow box. **CASE** *You explore the settings associated with your account, learn how to switch accounts, and sign out of an account.*

STEPS

1. **Sign in to Windows, if necessary, launch Word, click Blank document, then verify that your name appears in the top right corner of your screen**

2. **Click the list arrow to the right of your name, as shown in FIGURE WEB-4, then click About me and sign in if prompted**

   Internet Explorer opens and your Profile page appears. Here, you can add or edit your contact information and information about your workplace. You can also change the name and picture that appear in the top right corner of your window.

3. **Click the list arrow next to Profile in the top left corner of your screen, above the picture**

   The tiles representing the services your Windows account is connected to appear as shown in FIGURE WEB-5. Note that if you have connected your Microsoft account to accounts in other services such as Facebook, LinkedIn, or outlook.com, you will see these connections in the appropriate app. For example, your connections to Facebook and LinkedIn appear in the People app.

4. **Click a blank area below the apps tiles, click Your Name in the top right corner, then click Account settings**

   Either you are taken directly to the Microsoft account screen or, depending on your security settings, a Sign in screen appears. To make changes to your account, you might need to enter the password associated with your account. You can also choose to sign in with a different Microsoft account. Once you sign in, you can change the information associated with your account such as your name, email address, birth date, and password. You can also choose to close your Microsoft account, which deletes all the data associated with it.

5. **Click the Close button ✕ in the upper right corner of the window to remove the Sign-in window, click Close all tabs to return to Word, then click the list arrow ▼ next to Your Name in the top right corner of the Word window**

   To sign out of your account, you can click Sign Out at the top of the Accounts dialog box that appears when you click Account Settings. When you are working on your own computers, you will rarely need to sign out of your account. However, if you are working on a public computer, you may want to sign out of your account to avoid having your files accessible to other users.

6. **Click Switch account**

   You can choose to sign into another Microsoft account or to an account with an organization.

7. **Click the Close button ✕**

   You are returned to a blank document in Word.

8. **Exit Word**

FIGURE WEB-4: Viewing Windows account options in Word

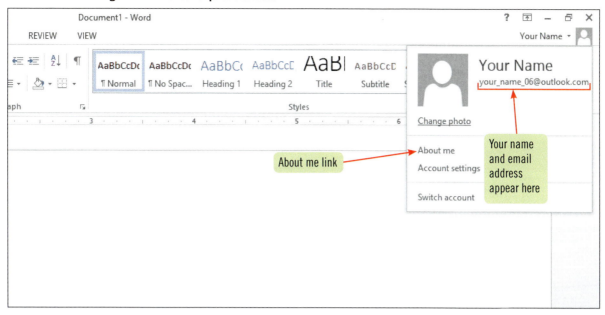

FIGURE WEB-5: Connected services associated with a Profile

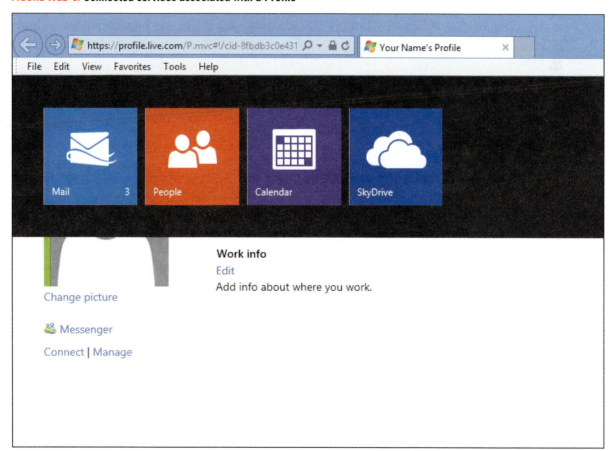

Cloud

Getting a Microsoft account

If you have been working with Windows and Office 2013, you might already have a Microsoft account, which was previously referred to as a Windows Live ID. You also have an account if you use outlook.com (formerly Hotmail), SkyDrive, Xbox LIVE, or have a Windows Phone. A Microsoft account consists of an email address and a password. If you wish to create a new Microsoft account, go to https://signup.live.com/ and follow the directions provided.

Working in the Cloud

Cloud 5

Explore SkyDrive

Learning Outcomes
• Save a file to SkyDrive
• Create a folder on SkyDrive

SkyDrive works like the hard drive on your computer. You can save and open files from SkyDrive, create folders, and manage your files. You can access the files you save on SkyDrive from any of your connected devices and from anywhere you have a computer connection. **CASE** *You open a PowerPoint presentation, save the file to your SkyDrive, then create a folder.*

STEPS

1. **Start PowerPoint, then open the file WEB-1.pptx from the location where you store your Data Files**

2. **Click the FILE tab, click Save As, then click Your Name's SkyDrive (top selection) if it is not already selected**

3. **Click the Browse button**

   The Save As dialog box opens, showing the folders stored on your SkyDrive. You may have several folders already stored there or you may have none.

4. **Click New folder, type Cengage, then press [Enter]**

5. **Double-click Cengage, select WEB-1.pptx in the File name text box, type WEB-QST Vancouver 1 as shown in FIGURE WEB-6, then click Save**

   The file is saved to the Cengage folder on the SkyDrive that is associated with your Microsoft account. The PowerPoint window reappears.

6. **Click the FILE tab, click Close, click the FILE tab, then click Open**

   WEB-QST Vancouver 1.pptx appears as the first file listed in the Recent Presentations list, and the path to your Cengage folder on your SkyDrive appears beneath it.

7. **Click WEB-QST Vancouver 1.pptx to open it, then type your name where indicated on the title slide**

8. **Click Slide 2 in the Navigation pane, select 20% in the third bullet, type 30%, click the FILE tab, click Save As, click Cengage under Current Folder, change the file name to WEB-QST Vancouver 2, then click Save**

9. **Exit PowerPoint**

   A new version of the presentation is saved to the Cengage folder that you created on SkyDrive.

How to disable default saving to Skydrive

You can specify how you want to save files from Office 2013 applications. By default, files are saved to locations you specify on your SkyDrive. You can change the default to be a different location. In Word, PowerPoint, or Excel, click the FILE tab, then click Options. Click Save in the left sidebar, then in the Save section, click the Save to Computer by default check box, as shown in **FIGURE WEB-7**. Click OK to close the PowerPoint Options dialog box. The Save options you've selected will be active in Word, PowerPoint, and Excel, regardless of which application you were using when you changed the option.

FIGURE WEB-6: Saving a presentation to SkyDrive

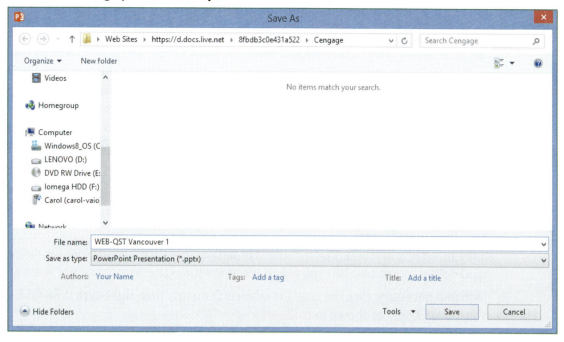

FIGURE WEB-7: Changing the default Save location in PowerPoint

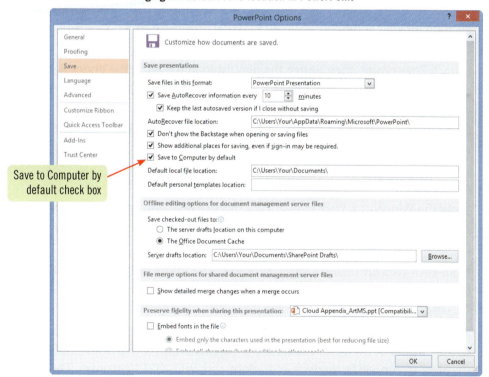

Save to Computer by
default check box

Cloud

Manage Files on SkyDrive

You are automatically connected to SkyDrive when you sign into your Microsoft account and launch an Office 2013 application. You can also access SkyDrive through your Web browser or from the SkyDrive App in Windows 8. When you start the SkyDrive App, you can upload and download files, create folders, and delete files. You can also download the SkyDrive app to your tablet or other mobile device so you can access files wherever you have an Internet connection. When you access SkyDrive from Internet Explorer, you can do more file management tasks, including renaming and moving files. **CASE** *You explore how to work with SkyDrive from your Web browser and from the SkyDrive App.*

STEPS

1. **Launch Internet Explorer or another Web browser, type skydrive.com in the Address box, then press [Enter]**

   If you are signed in to your Microsoft account, your SkyDrive opens. If you are not signed in, the login page appears where you can enter the email address and password associated with your Microsoft account.

2. **Sign in if necessary, click the blue tile labeled Cengage, then right-click WEB-QST Vancouver 1.pptx as shown in FIGURE WEB-8**

   You can open the file in the PowerPoint Web App or in PowerPoint, download the file to your computer, share it, embed it, and perform other actions such as renaming and deleting.

3. **Click Download, click Open in the bar at the bottom of the screen, then click Enable Editing**

   The presentation opens in PowerPoint where you can save it to your computer hard drive or back to SkyDrive.

4. **Click the DESIGN tab, click the More button ▼ in the Themes group, select the Wisp theme, click the FILE tab, click Save As, click Computer, click Browse, navigate to a location on your computer or on an external drive such as a USB flash drive, click Save, then exit PowerPoint**

5. **Launch PowerPoint, then notice the files listed in the left pane under Recent**

   The file you just saved to your computer or external drive appears first and the file saved to the Cengage folder on SkyDrive appears second.

6. **Click the second listing, notice that the file is not updated with the Wisp design, then exit PowerPoint**

   When you download a file from SkyDrive, changes you make are not saved to the version on SkyDrive. You can also access SkyDrive from your Windows 8 screen by using the SkyDrive app.

7. **Show the Windows 8 Start screen, click the SkyDrive tile, open the Cengage folder, right-click WEB-QST Vancouver 1, view the buttons on the taskbar as shown in FIGURE WEB-9, click the Delete button on the taskbar, then click Delete**

8. **Right-click WEB-QST Vancouver 2, click the New Folder button on the taskbar, type Illustrated, then click Create folder**

   You can rename and move files in SkyDrive through Internet Explorer.

9. **Move the mouse pointer to the top of the screen until it becomes the hand pointer, drag to the bottom of the screen to close the SkyDrive App, click the Internet Explorer tile on the Start screen, go to skydrive.com, right-click WEB-QST Vancouver 2 on the SkyDrive site, click Move to, click the ▶ next to Cengage, click Illustrated, then click Move**

FIGURE WEB-8: File management options on SkyDrive

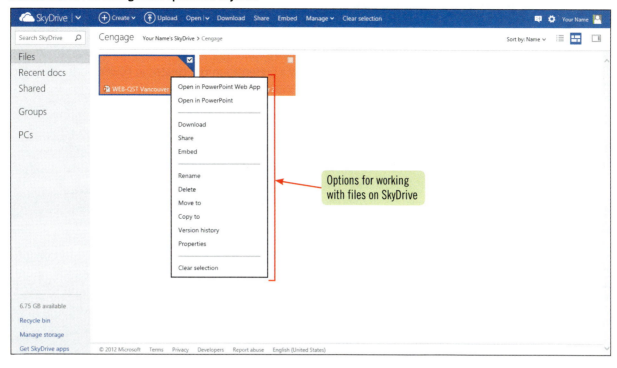

Options for working with files on SkyDrive

FIGURE WEB-9: File management options on SkyDrive App

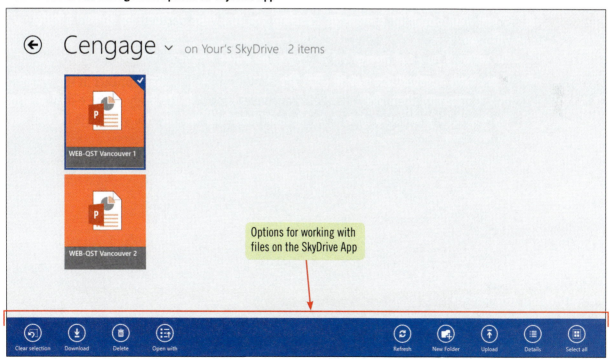

Options for working with files on the SkyDrive App

Cloud

Share Files

**Learning
Outcome**
• Share a file from
SkyDrive

One of the great advantages of working with SkyDrive is that you can share your files with others. Suppose, for example, that you want a colleague to review a presentation you created in PowerPoint and then add a new slide. You can, of course, e-mail the presentation directly to your colleague who can then make changes and e-mail the presentation back. Alternatively, you can share the PowerPoint file directly from SkyDrive. Your colleague can edit the file using the PowerPoint Web App or the full version of PowerPoint, and then you can check the updated file on SkyDrive. In this way, you and your colleague are working with just one version of the presentation that you both can update. **CASE** *You have decided to share files in the Illustrated folder that you created in the previous lesson with another individual. You start by sharing files with your partner and your partner can share files with you.*

STEPS

TROUBLE
If you cannot find a partner, you can email the file to yourself.

1. **Identify a partner with whom you can work, and obtain his or her e-mail address; you can choose someone in your class or someone on your e-mail list, but it should be some-one who will be completing these steps when you are**

2. **Right-click the Illustrated folder, then click Sharing as shown in FIGURE WEB-10**

3. **Type the e-mail address of your partner**

4. **Click in the Include a personal message box, then type Here's the presentation we're working on together as shown in FIGURE WEB-11**

5. **Verify that the Recipients can edit check box is selected, then click Share**
   Your partner will receive a message advising him or her that you have shared the WEB-QST Vancouver 2.pptx file. If your partner is completing the steps at the same time, you will receive an e-mail from your partner.

TROUBLE
If you do not receive a message, your partner has not yet completed the steps to share the folder.

6. **Check your e-mail for a message advising you that your partner has shared a folder with you**
   The subject of the e-mail message will be "[Name] has shared documents with you."

7. **If you have received the e-mail, click the Show content link that appears in the warning box, if necesary, then click WEB-QST Vancouver 2.pptx in the body of the e-mail message**
   The PowerPoint presentation opens in the Microsoft PowerPoint Web App. You will work in the Web App in the next lesson.

Co-authoring documents

You can work on a document, presentation, or workbook simultaneously with a partner. First, save the file to your SkyDrive. Click the FILE tab, click Share, then click Invite People. Enter the email addresses of the people you want to work on the file with you and then click Share. Once your partner has received, opened, and started editing the document, you can start working together. You will see a notification in the status bar that someone is editing the document with you. When you click the notification, you can see the name of the other user and their picture if they have one attached to their Windows account. When your partner saves, you'll see his or changes in green shading which goes away the next time you save. You'll have an opportunity to co-author documents when you complete the Team Project at the end of this appendix.

FIGURE WEB-10: Sharing a file from SkyDrive

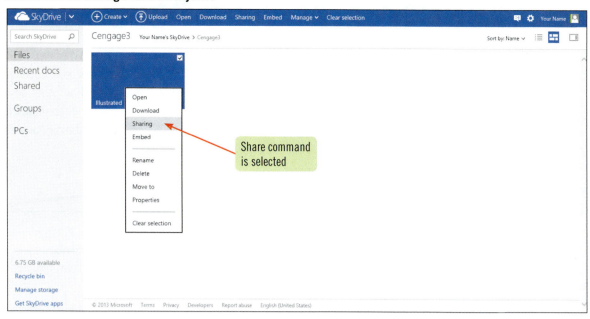

FIGURE WEB-11: Sharing a file with another person

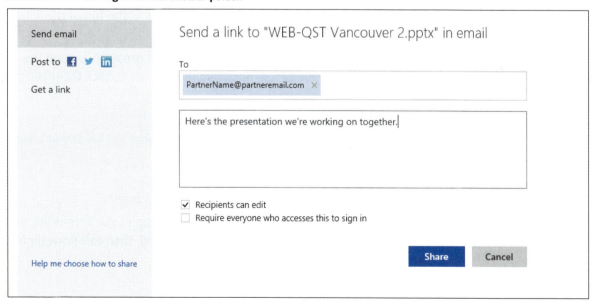

Explore Office Web Apps

Learning Outcomes
- Edit a presentation with PowerPoint Web App
- Open a presentation from PowerPoint Web App

As you have learned, a Web App is a scaled-down version of an Office program. Office Web Apps include Word, Excel, PowerPoint, and OneNote. You can use the Office Web Apps to create and edit documents even if you don't have Office 2013 installed on your computer and you can use them on other devices such as tablets and smartphones. From SkyDrive, you can also open the document in the full Office application if the application is installed on the computer you are using. **CASE** ▶ *You use the PowerPoint Web App and the full version of PowerPoint to edit the presentation.*

STEPS

1. **Click EDIT PRESENTATION, then click Edit in PowerPoint Web App**

   Presentations opened using the PowerPoint Web App have the same look and feel as presentations opened using the full version of PowerPoint. However, like all of the Office Web Apps, the PowerPoint Web App has fewer features available than the full version of PowerPoint.

2. **Review the Ribbon and its tabs to familiarize yourself with the commands you can access from the PowerPoint Web App**

   TABLE WEB-1 summarizes the commands that are available.

   TROUBLE
   You need to click the text first, click it again, then drag to select it.

3. **Click Slide 3, click the text Hornby Island, click it again and select it, then type Tofino so the bullet item reads Tofino Sea Kayaking**

4. **Click outside the text box, click the DESIGN tab, then click the More Themes list arrow ▼ to show the selection of designs available**

   A limited number of designs are available on the PowerPoint Web App. When you want to use a design or a command that is not available on the PowerPoint Web App, you open the file in the full version of PowerPoint.

5. **Click on a blank area of the slide, click OPEN IN POWERPOINT at the top of the window, then click Yes in response to the message**

6. **Click the DESIGN tab, click the More button ▼ in the Themes group to expand the Themes gallery, select the Quotable design as shown in FIGURE WEB-12, click the picture on Slide 1, then press [Delete]**

7. **Click the Save button 🖫 on the Quick Access toolbar**

   The Save button includes a small icon indicating you are saving to SkyDrive and not to your computer's hard drive or an external drive.

8. **Click the Close button ✕ to exit PowerPoint**

   You open the document again to verify that your partner made the same changes.

9. **Launch PowerPoint, click WEB-QST Vancouver 2.pptx at the top of the Recent list, verify that the Quotable design is applied and the picture is removed, then exit PowerPoint**

Exploring other Office Web Apps

Three other Office Web Apps are Word, Excel, and OneNote. You can share files on SkyDrive directly from any of these applications using the same method you used to share files from PowerPoint. To familiarize yourself with the commands available in an Office Web App, open the file and then review the commands on each tab on the Ribbon. If you want to perform a task that is not available in the Web App, open the file in the full version of the application.

FIGURE WEB-12: Selecting the Quotable design

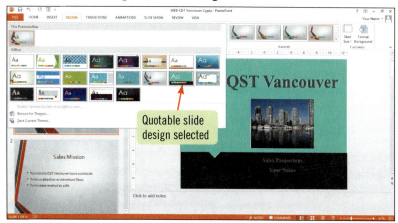

Quotable slide design selected

TABLE WEB-1: Commands on the PowerPoint Web App

tab	category/group	options
FILE	Info	• Open in PowerPoint (also available on the toolbar above the document window)
		• Previous Versions
	Save As	• Where's the Save Button?: In PowerPoint Web App, the presentation is being saved automatically so there is no Save button
		• Download: use to download a copy of the presentation to your computer
	Print	• Create a printable PDF of the presentation that you can then open and print
	Share	• Share with people - you can invite others to view and edit your presentation
		• Embed - include the presentation in a blog on Web site
	About	• Try Microsoft Office, Terms of Use, and Privacy and Cookies
	Help	• Help with PowerPoint questions, Give Feedback to Microsoft, and modify how you can view the presentation (for example, text only)
	Exit	• Close the presentation and exit to view SkyDrive folders
HOME	Clipboard	• Cut, Copy, Paste, Format Painter
	Delete	• Delete a slide
	Slides	• Add a new slide, duplicate a slide, hide a slide
	Font	• Change the font, size, style, and color of selected text
	Paragraph	• Add bullets and numbering, indent text, align text, and change text direction
	Drawing	• Add text boxes and shapes, arrange them on the slide, apply Quick Styles, modify shape fill and outline, and duplicate a shape
INSERT	Slides	• Add new slides with selected layout
	Images	• Add pictures from your computer, online pictures, or screen shots
	Illustrations	• Add shapes, SmartArt, or charts
	Links	• Add links or actions to objects
	Text	• Add comments, text boxes, headers and footers, and other text elements
	Comments	• Add comments
DESIGN	Themes	• Apply a limited number of themes to a presentation and apply variants to a selected theme
		• Apply variants to a selected theme
ANIMATIONS	Animation	• Apply a limited number of animation effects to a slide element and modify existing timings
TRANSITIONS	Transitions to This Slide	• Apply a limited number of transition effects to slides and chose to apply the effect to all slides
VIEW	Presentation Views	• You can view the slide in Editing View, Reading View, Slide Show View, and Notes View and you can show any comments made by users who worked on PowerPoint using the full version

Cloud

Team Project

Introduction

From SkyDrive, you can easily collaborate with others to produce documents, presentations, and spreadsheets that include each user's input. Instead of emailing a document to colleagues and then waiting for changes, you can both work on the document at the same time online. To further explore how you can work with SkyDrive and Office 2013, you will work with two other people to complete a team project. The subject of the team project is the planning of a special event of your choice, such as a class party, a lecture, or a concert. The special event should be limited to a single afternoon or evening.

Follow the guidelines provided below to create the files required for the team project. When you have completed the project, the team will submit a Word document containing information about your project, as well as three files related to the project: a Word document, a PowerPoint presentation, and an Excel workbook.

Project Setup

As a team, work together to complete the following tasks.

a. Share email addresses among all three team members.

b. Set up a time (either via email, an online chat session, Internet Messaging, or face to face) when you will get together to choose your topic and assign roles.

c. At your meeting, complete the table below with information about your team and your special event.

Team Name (last name of one team member or another name that describes the project.)
Team Members
Event type (for example, party, lecture, concert, etc.)
Event purpose (for example, fundraiser for a specific cause, celebrate the end of term, feature a special guest, etc.)
Event location, date, and time
Team Roles indicate who is responsible for each of the following three files (one file per team member)
Word document:
Excel workbook:
PowerPoint presentation:

Document Development

Individually, complete the tasks listed below for the file you are responsible for. You need to develop appropriate content, format the file attractively, and then be prepared to share the file with the other team members.

Word Document

The Word document contains a description of your special event and includes a table listing responsibilities and a time line. Create the Word document as follows:

1. Create a Cloud Project folder on your SkyDrive, then create a new Word document and save it as **Cloud Project_ Word Description** to the Cloud Project folder.

Document Development (continued)

2. Include a title with the name of your project and a subtitle with the names of your team members. Format the title with the Title style and the subtitle with the Subtitle style.

3. Write a paragraph describing the special event—its topics, purpose, the people involved, etc. You can paraphrase some of the information your team discussed in your meeting.

4. Create a table similar to the table shown below and then complete it with the required information. Include up to ten rows. A task could be "Contact the caterers" or "Pick up the speaker." Visualize the sequence of tasks required to put on the event.

Task	Person Responsible	Deadline

5. Format the table using the table style of your choice.

6. Save the document to your SkyDrive. You will share the document with your team members and receive feedback in the next section.

Excel Workbook

The Excel workbook contains a budget for the special event. Create the Excel workbook as follows:

1. Create a new Excel workbook and save it as **Cloud Project_Excel Budget** to the Cloud Project folder on your SkyDrive.

2. Create a budget that includes both the revenues you expect from the event (for example, ticket sales, donations, etc.) and the expenses. Expense items include advertising costs (posters, ads, etc.), food costs if the event is catered, transportation costs, etc. The revenues and expenses you choose will depend upon the nature of the project.

3. Make the required calculations to total all the revenue items and all the expense items.

4. Calculate the net profit (or loss) as the revenue minus the expenses.

5. Format the budget attractively using fill colors, border lines, and other enhancements to make the data easy to read.

6. Save the workbook to your SkyDrive. You will share the workbook with your team members and receive feedback in the next section.

PowerPoint Presentation

The PowerPoint presentation contains a presentation that describes the special event to an audience who may be interested in attending. Create the PowerPoint presentation as follows:

1. Create a new PowerPoint presentation and save it as **Cloud Project_PowerPoint Presentation** to the Cloud Project folder on your SkyDrive.

2. Create a presentation that consists of five slides including the title slide as follows:

   a. Slide 1: Title slide includes the name of the event and your team members

   b. Slide 2: Purpose of the party or event

   c. Slide 3: Location, time, and cost

   d. Slide 4: Chart showing a breakdown of costs (to be supplied when you co-author in the next section)

   e. Slide 5: Motivational closing slide designed to encourage the audience to attend; include appropriate pictures

3. Format the presentation attractively using the theme of your choice.

4. Save the presentation to your SkyDrive. You will share the presentation with your team members and receive feedback.

Co-Authoring on Skydrive

You need to share your file, add feedback to the other two files, then create a final version of your file. When you read the file created by the other two team members, you need to add additional data or suggestions. For example, if you created the Excel budget, you can provide the person who created the PowerPoint presentation with information about the cost break-down. If you created the Word document, you can add information about the total revenue and expenses contained in the Excel budget to your description. You decide what information to add to each of the two files you work with.

1. Open the file you created.
2. Click the **FILE tab**, click **Share**, then click **Invite People**.
3. Enter the email addresses of the other two team members, then enter the following message: **Here's the file I created for our team project. Please make any changes, provide suggestions, and then save it. Thanks!** See **FIGURE WEB-13**.

FIGURE WEB-13

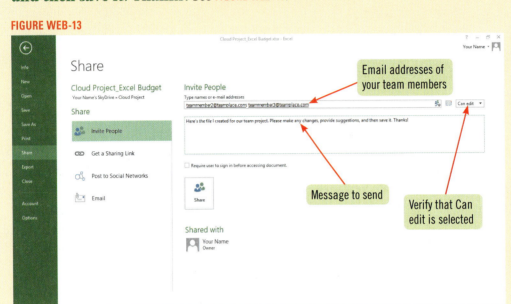

4. Click the **Share button**.
5. Allow team members time to add information and comments to your file. Team members should save frequently. When the file is saved, it is saved directly to your SkyDrive. Note that you can work together on the document or you can work separately. You can also choose to make changes with the full version of the Office 2013 applications or with the Office Web Apps. When someone is working on your file, you will see their user name on the status bar.
6. Decide which changes you want to keep, make any further changes you think are needed to make the document as clear as possible, then save a final version.

Project Summary

When you are pleased with the contents of your file and have provided feedback to your team members, assign a team member to complete the following tasks and then complete your portion as required.

1. Open **WEB-2.docx** from the location where you save your Data Files, then save it to your Cloud Project folder on your SkyDrive as **Cloud Project_Summary**.
2. Read the directions in the document, then enter your name as Team Member 1 and write a short description of your experience working with SkyDrive and Office 2013 to complete the team project.
3. Share the file with your team members and request that they add their own names and descriptions.
4. When all team members have finished working on the document, save all the changes.
5. Make sure you store all four files completed for the project in the Cloud Project appendix on your SkyDrive, then submit them to your instructor on behalf of your team.

Glossary

Active cell The selected cell in a worksheet.

Adjustment handle A small yellow handle that changes the appearance of an object's most prominent feature.

Align To place objects' edges or centers on the same plane.

Animation tag Identifies the order an object is animated on a slide during a slide show.

Annotate A freehand drawing on the screen made by using the pen or highlighter tool. You can annotate only in Slide Show view.

Background The area behind the text and graphics on a slide.

Background graphic An object placed on the slide master.

Category axis The axis in a chart that contains the categories or labels defining the data series.

Cell The intersection of a column and row in a worksheet, or table.

Chart A graphical representation of numerical data from a worksheet. Chart types include 2-D and 3-D column, bar, pie, area, and line charts.

Cloud computing When data, applications, and resources are stored on servers accessed over the Internet or a company's internal network rather than on user's computers.

Column heading The box containing the column letter on top of the columns in the worksheet.

Content placeholder A placeholder that is used to enter text or objects such as clip art, charts, or pictures.

Comments button A button on the PowerPoint status bar in Normal view allows you to open the Comments pane where you can create, edit, select, and delete comments.

Crop To hide part of an object, such as using the Cropping tool or to delete a part of a picture.

Data series A column or row in a worksheet.

Data series label Text in the first row and column of a worksheet that identifies data in a chart.

Data series marker A graphical representation of a data series, such as a bar or column.

Destination presentation The presentation you insert slides to when you reuse slides from another presentation.

Digital signature A way to authenticate a presentation files using computer cryptography. A digital signature is not visible in a presentation.

Distribute To evenly divide the space horizontally or vertically between objects relative to each other or the slide edges.

Document Inspector A PowerPoint feature that examines a presentation for hidden data or personal information.

Embedded object An object that is created in one application and inserted to another; can be edited using the original program file in which they were created.

Gallery A visual collection of choices you can browse through to make a selection. Often available with Live Preview.

Gridlines Evenly spaced horizontal and vertical lines on the slide that help you align objects.

Group A PowerPoint feature in which you combine multiple objects into one object.

Groups Areas of the Ribbon that arrange commands based on their function, for example, text formatting commands such as Bold, Underline, and Italic are located on the HOME tab, in the Font group.

Insertion point A blinking vertical line that indicates where the next character will appear when text is entered in a text placeholder in PowerPoint.

Legend Text box feature in a chart that provides an explanation about the data presented in a chart.

Live Preview A feature that shows you the result of an action such as a theme change before you apply the change.

Masters One of three views that stores information about the presentation theme, fonts, placeholders, and other background objects. The three master views are Slide Master view, Handout Master view, and Notes Master view.

Merge A feature in PowerPoint used to combine multiple shapes together; provides you a way to create a variety of unique geometric shapes that are not available in the Shapes gallery.

Metadata Another name for document properties that includes the author name, the document subject, the document title, and other personal information.

Mini toolbar A small toolbar that appears next to selected text that contains basic text-formatting commands.

Normal view The primary view that you use to write, edit, and design your presentation. Normal view is divided into three panes: Thumbnails, Slide, and Notes.

Notes button A button on the status bar in PowerPoint that opens the Notes pane.

Notes Page view A presentation view that displays a reduced image of the current slide above a large text box where you can type notes.

Notes pane The area in Normal view that shows speaker notes for the current slide; also in Notes Page view, the area below the slide image that contains speaker notes.

Object An item you place or draw on a slide that can be modified. Examples of objects include drawn lines and shapes, text, and imported pictures.

Office Web App Versions of the Microsoft Office applications with limited functionality that are available online from Windows Live SkyDrive. Users can view documents online and then edit them in the browser using a selection of functions.

Online collaboration The ability to incorporate feedback or share information across the Internet or a company network or intranet.

Outline view A view in PowerPoint where you can enter text on slides in outline form.

Pane A section of the PowerPoint window, such as the Slide or Thumbnails pane.

Picture A digital photograph, piece of line art, or other graphic that is created in another program and is inserted into PowerPoint.

PowerPoint window A window that contains the running PowerPoint application. The PowerPoint window includes the Ribbon, panes, and Presentation window.

Presentation software A software program used to organize and present information typically as part of an electronic slide show.

Presenter view A PowerPoint view you access while in Slide Show view. Typically you use this view when showing a presentation through two monitors, one that you see as the presenter and one that the audience sees.

Previewing Prior to printing, seeing onscreen exactly how the printed document will look.

Quick Access toolbar A small toolbar on the left side of a Microsoft application program window's title bar, containing buttons that you click to quickly perform common actions, such as saving a file.

Quick Style Determines how fonts, colors, and effects of the theme are combined and which color, font, and effect is dominant. A Quick Style can be applied to shapes or text.

Reading view A view you use to review your presentation or present a slide show to someone on a computer monitor.

Read-only A file that can't be edited or modified.

Ribbon A wide band of buttons spanning the top of the PowerPoint window that organizes all of PowerPoint's primary commands.

Rotate handle A small round arrow at the top of a selected object that you can drag to rotate the selected object.

Row heading The box containing the row number to the left of the row in a worksheet.

Screen capture An electronic snapshot of your screen, as if you took a picture of it with a camera, which you can paste into a document.

Selection box A dashed border that appears around a text object or placeholder, indicating that it is ready to accept text.

Sizing handles The small squares that appear around a selected object. Dragging a sizing handle resizes the object.

SkyDrive An online storage and file sharing service. Access to SkyDrive is through a Windows Live account.

Slide layout This determines how all of the elements on a slide are arranged, including text and content placeholders.

Slide library A folder that you and others can access to open, modify, and review presentation slides.

Slide pane The main section of Normal view that displays the current slide.

Slide Show view A view that shows a presentation as an electronic slide show; each slide fills the screen.

Slide Sorter view A view that displays a thumbnail of all slides in the order in which they appear in your presentation; used to rearrange slides and slide transitions.

Slide thumbnail *See* Thumbnail.

Slide timing The amount of time each slide is visible on the screen during a slide show.

Slide transition The special effect that moves one slide off the screen and the next slide on the screen during a slide show. Each slide can have its own transition effect.

SmartArt A professional quality graphic diagram that visually illustrates text.

SmartArt Style A pre-set combination of formatting options that follows the design theme that you can apply to a SmartArt graphic.

Smart Guides A feature in PowerPoint used to help position objects relative to each other and determine equal distances between objects.

Source presentation The presentation you insert slides from when you reuse slides from another presentation.

Status bar The bar at the bottom of the PowerPoint window that contains messages about what you are doing and seeing in PowerPoint, such as the current slide number or the current theme.

Subtitle text placeholder A box on the title slide reserved for subpoint text.

Tab A section of the Ribbon that identifies groups of commands like the HOME tab.

Text placeholder A box with a dotted border and text that you replace with your own text.

Theme A set of colors, fonts, and effects that you apply to a presentation from the Themes Gallery.

Theme colors The set of 12 coordinated colors that make up a PowerPoint presentation; a theme assigns colors for text, lines, fills, accents, hyperlinks, and background.

Theme effects The set of effects for lines and fills.

Theme fonts The set of fonts for titles and other text.

Thumbnail A small image of a slide. Thumbnails are visible on the Thumbnails pane and in Slide Sorter view.

Thumbnails pane On the left side of the Normal view, used to quickly navigate through the slides in your presentation by clicking the thumbnails on this pane.

Title placeholder A box on a slide reserved for the title of a presentation or slide.

Title slide The first slide in a presentation.

Value axis The axis in a chart that contains the values or numbers defining the data series.

Variant A custom variation of the applied theme that uses different colors, fonts, and effects.

View A way of displaying a presentation, such as Normal view, Reading view, Notes Page view, Slide Sorter view, and Slide Show view.

View Shortcuts The buttons at the bottom of the PowerPoint window on the status bar that you click to switch among views.

Windows Live A collection of services and Web applications that people can access through a login. Windows Live services include access to email and instant messaging, storage of files on SkyDrive, sharing and storage of photos, networking with people, downloading software, and interfacing with a mobile device.

WordArt A set of decorative styles or text effects that is applied to text.

Worksheet The grid of rows and columns that stores the numerical data for a chart.

XML Acronym that stands for eXtensible Markup Language, which is a language used to structure, store, and send information.

Zoom slider A feature on the status bar that allows you to change the zoom percentage of a slide.

Index